THE
19

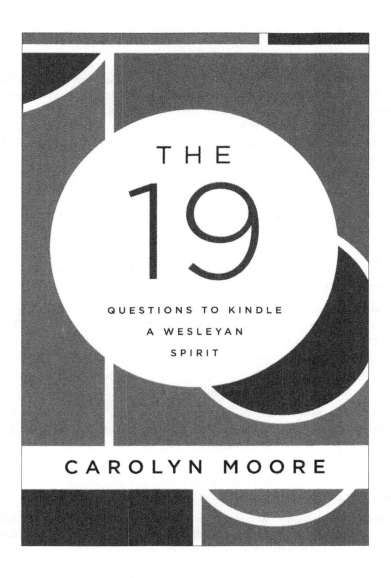

THE
19

QUESTIONS TO KINDLE

A WESLEYAN

SPIRIT

CAROLYN MOORE

Abingdon Press / Nashville

THE 19
QUESTIONS TO KINDLE A WESLEYAN SPIRIT

This book is printed on elemental chlorine-free paper.
ISBN 978-1-5018-61093

18 19 20 21 22 23 24 25 26 27 — 10 9 8 7 6 5 4 3 2 1
MANUFACTURED IN THE UNITED STATES OF AMERICA

CONTENTS

THE

19

QUESTIONS TO KINDLE
A WESLEYAN
SPIRIT

INTRODUCTION:
THEOLOGY WITH A QUESTION MARK

The problem is that Jesus rarely answers the question you ask him.

"By what authority," asked a few skeptical leaders of the synagogue, "are you doing these miracles and teaching these lessons?" In other words, "Who do you think you are?"

Jesus answered by asking a question. "I'll tell you by whose authority I do these things," he said, "but first let me ask you something. Did the baptism of John come from heaven, or was it of human origin?"

It was one of those puzzles only an expert can answer. It was a challenge and a lesson dressed up as a question. It called them out as unfaithful, no matter which answer they gave. If John's authority was from heaven, they were exposed as rebellious because they hadn't believed him. If they said his authority was from earth, they risked the ire of the crowds who followed John as a prophet. Learned though they were, they couldn't tease out an answer that didn't condemn them.

"Well, then," Jesus shrugged, "I won't answer your question, either" (see Matthew 21:23-27).

Brilliant.

Another time, the religious leaders came to Jesus after they noticed his disciples weren't washing their hands before meals—a big deal in their tradition. Why couldn't Jesus' followers play by the traditional rules? Again,

Jesus answered by not answering. Why, he wondered, didn't they take better care of their parents? Why didn't they follow the Jewish rules of compassion and honor? (Matthew 15:1-6)

Jesus asked a lot of questions. Three-hundred seven, to be exact. He only answered three.[1] I'm thinking Jesus was onto something.

- "Do you want to get well?" (John 5:6)
- "If you love those who love you, what reward will you get?" (Matthew 5:46)
- "Since you do not believe what [Moses] wrote, how are you going to believe what I say?" (John 5:47)

A great question has power. A question mark is almost like a trowel. It dips into the soil of our hearts and churns up latent feelings or beliefs we didn't even know were there. A great question can stop us in our tracks and change our perspective. Good answers fix problems in the short term. Good questions have the power to create lasting change. *Great* questions can change a worldview.

Asking good questions was a technique John Wesley used. A devout student of "The Book," surely he learned that skill from the best of the best.

The questions his Holy Club asked and answered were designed to expose the souls of those who participated in weekly accountability, and those questions still have power to expose our weaknesses and call us to account for making spiritual progress. Wesley developed similar avenues for accountability in the Methodist class and band meetings, which also used questions to help people grow in faith.

Beyond those accountability questions in the Holy Club and in class and band meetings, Wesley developed nineteen other questions to probe the hearts and motives of potential Methodist preachers. These questions have had a kind of staying power. Since the 1700s, pastors in the United Methodist tradition have answered these nineteen historic questions as a way of agreeing to how we will live into this ministry life. Candidates for ordination examine these questions and prepare to answer them at the annual conference during which they are ordained.[2] It is the beginning point of our connection.

For Conscience' Sake

Do you wonder why Wesley chose questions? Why not statements of faith or something that sounds more like a manifesto? Was his choice an act of practicality or a stroke of brilliance? I suspect the latter. Because he chose to ask questions of those seeking to lead in the early Methodist movement, pastors for nearly 250 years have had their worldview shaped, their calling clarified, and their potential unearthed by these nineteen potent ideas presented as theological affirmations with a question mark.

By the time an ordinand stands to answer these questions publicly, he or she has already been approved for ministry. An appointment has already been chosen. The candidate's family has arrived from out of town to celebrate the milestone. No one reasonably expects the candidate to answer in a way that would preclude ordination. Much like a wedding, while the public profession is authentic, the commitment seems to have been made long before the big day.

And much like a wedding, one might well answer these important questions faithfully on the "big day," then quickly forget the substance of them in the years to follow.

I read these questions for the first time when I was preparing for ordination. After that, I can't say that I so much as thought about most of them again until almost twenty years after I first answered them publicly. I pulled them out in recent years when conflicts within The United Methodist Church began to heat up and pointed questions were being leveled at opposing "sides" about what matters theologically. As a blogger, I was surprised to find some of those questions leveled at me. I have had people take issue with my use of the term *orthodoxy*, informing me that I don't get to decide what orthodoxy means. I would agree. Neither I nor they get to decide what it means. Orthodoxy *has* an accepted meaning. *Methodism* is another term I'm hearing tossed about as if it too can be redefined according to whim and culture. And *love*. Evidently, some circles get to define what love is, while others are labeled as unloving or unjust by virtue of their disagreement with those definitions.

As the debates and contemporary questions swirl, I'm drawn back to these historic nineteen questions. In them, I've discovered something unexpected and sublime. I've found that rather than becoming distant and lifeless, these questions have only been enriched by time. After twenty years of ministry, I now have experience to support their richness. I understand freshly that knowing what you believe matters. In light of denominational turmoil, I recognize the importance of publicly committing to our doctrines. In these questions, I hear the heart of a man at the helm of a new and growing movement. When he asked his candidates whether they were resolved, whether they were earnest, whether they would study and be diligent in instructing others, Wesley wasn't after company men or career women. He was looking for fruitful, whole-hearted followers of Jesus willing to give their all to this Methodist way. It was his vision that these questions both inspire and require a cohesive unity—one heart, one mind, one mission.

Unfortunately, the issues facing us in this age are leading us in opposing directions. The issues of marriage, sexuality, and ordination have polarized clergy and laity alike. For some of my clergy colleagues, upholding and supporting United Methodism's traditional view of marriage and sexuality is a violation of their conscience. For other colleagues of mine, their conscience is violated when they sense a lack of accountability on the part of progressive clergy and leaders (when, for example, a same-sex union is performed by a United Methodist minister and there is no ministerial consequence).

Countless conversations have tried in vain to find the common ground between these two "sides." I suggest that we are searching for common ground in the wrong field. It won't be found in our widely diverse opinions on social issues. Instead, these nineteen questions define the ground on which the foundation of Methodism was built—Christ, Scripture, doctrine, polity, our rules, spiritual discipline. Those who can honestly, transparently examine their own heart on these matters should be able to decide for themselves if this is their tribe, and these questions are an able guide. Much more than a test on the way to ordination, these questions were—and are—a kind of spiritual and doctrinal accountability. They are meant to live in us, to be lived out much as Paul advised us to work out our salvation daily with fear and trembling. They sound a call to faithful living and personal conviction.

Wesley tips his hand in the final phrase of his final question: "And do not mend our rules, but keep them; not for wrath, but for conscience' sake."

This line raises the bar to the level of personal holiness. This current division is indeed a matter of conscience, and for Wesley that was quite the point. By asking questions rather than barking decrees, the founder of this movement challenged all who would lead to *own* this, freely—*for conscience' sake*, he counsels. These profound and weighty questions are designed not to stamp out doctrinal robots, but to shape pastors and people who live, work, and minister with integrity—from a right heart, with authority, without fear, freely rather than under compulsion.

Those who choose to answer these questions in the pursuit of spiritual leadership should not have to be corralled into line behind them. Rather, they ought to be those who so thoroughly walk in the way of Jesus and in the spirit of a Methodist that these concepts become more of a challenge than a test, an inspiration to follow hard after our great redeemer, friend, and teacher, the Lord Jesus Christ.

In the request that these questions be rehearsed year after year, century after century, Wesley's motive was surely to produce men and women of God who were honestly, earnestly attempting to grow up in every way into Christ who is our head. If indeed that is the heart behind these questions (as I suspect), then they are worth asking of every United Methodist everywhere who seeks to live in covenanted connection with others around the globe who claim this Wesleyan theology as they seek to follow Jesus.

Wondering if you are up for that challenge? Spend time with these questions. Hear them as if spoken from the mouth of a man who sacrificed rather significantly for the cause of Christ and who has helped generations of Christians live out a practical theology of grace and truth.

---

1 Martin B. Copenhaver, *Jesus Is the Question: The 307 Questions Jesus Asked and the 3 He Answered* (Nashville: Abingdon Press, 2014).

2 *The Book of Discipline of The United Methodist Church 2016* (Nashville: The United Methodist Publishing House, 2016), ¶330 and 336, pp. 257–58 and 270–71.

THE

19

QUESTIONS TO KINDLE
A WESLEYAN
SPIRIT

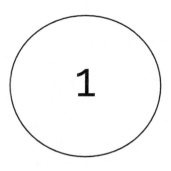

HAVE YOU FAITH IN CHRIST?

Well, do you?

What a bold question! It is especially bold when you consider these nineteen were designed not for confirmation of sixth graders or welcoming of new members, but as gatekeepers for potential preachers. Even with leaders in the movement, Wesley began with the most fundamental question of salvation: Have you faith in Christ?

I suspect Wesley knew human nature. He knew that even the best among us can fake it in ministry and do a lot of damage in the process. As much as we'd like to trust that every person who expresses a call to ministry is full of faith and passion for Jesus, experience tells us there are far too many stories of burned-out pastors drowning in crises of their own making years into their ministry. Faith in Christ is not a "given" for men and women who preach it; and without it, ministry is nothing more than clanging cymbals or a noisy gong.

Read the question again: Have you faith in Christ?

There are two operative words here: faith and Christ. Let's look closely at both of these.

Faith

Faith is not the absence of doubt; it is the presence of trust. Faith says that whether or not I understand all the details, whether or not I can comprehend all the theology, I will begin to follow and let assurance come as it will. In that way, faith is self-giving. It is an expression of love toward the object of my faith that takes me beyond myself.

Faith binds us. The story of Abraham that includes the near-sacrifice of Isaac is known in Judaism as the *Akedah*, a Hebrew word that means "binding." The word comes from Abraham's act of binding Isaac before placing him on the altar. There is an immense display of trust and obedience in this scene. A man goes beyond reason and lays down on an altar what he loves most, while a son trusts his father beyond what he can see. This is the essence of faith. It is a different kind of knowing. Some things only make sense if the path from A to B comes off the page and makes contact with the character of God. If this is true, it means there is another dimension of seeing that makes our world make sense. I want to call that dimension the dimension of faith, and I actually believe it is a higher form of knowing.

In Christ

But of course, Wesley is not asking us to have a generic faith with no concern for its target. "Have you faith in *Christ*?" he asks. This is the mark of a Methodist: Faith is the life of Christ living itself out in me. To trust in Christ is to believe who he himself claimed to be: the way, the truth and the life. He claimed to be the singular path to the heart of the Father and did not give us another option. To be Methodist is to believe in Jesus as redeemer of the world. Jesus, who we believe to be the Son of God, gave up his place as God to become a man and lived a sinless human life. He was and is all God, all human, fulfilling hundreds of prophecies written hundreds of years before he came. Isaiah 53 says it was the will of the Lord to crush him. Isaiah 61 tells us the Spirit of the Lord was upon him to bring good news to the poor, to bind up the brokenhearted, to proclaim freedom to the captives, and to open the prisons of those who are bound. As Isaiah prophesied, Jesus healed sick people, gave sight to blind people, raised a few dead people, and fed a lot of hungry people.

Jesus ate with sinners. United Methodists were the first ones to add that line to the liturgy of our Eucharist. It matters to us that Jesus was that kind of Messiah. He lived a thoroughly compassionate life and the whole time, he talked about the kingdom of God and about how in the Kingdom we are forgiven our sins and made holy. Then Jesus became the sinless sacrifice that makes us holy. Because he had lived this sinless life, he became what they called in the Old Testament system of sacrifices a spotless lamb. Jesus gave himself to this. He allowed a group of men who were against everything he stood for to arrest him. They accused him of blasphemy because he claimed to be God.

Have you faith in that Christ? No one answering this question in the affirmative has a right to soften its meaning for the sake of convenience or conscience. *I am convinced that this is the most fundamental dividing line in the United Methodist Church.* It is what we do with Christ.

Long before we part ways on issues of human sexuality or liturgical forms, we are already deeply and tragically divided at the point of Wesley's first question. Some among us want to claim a form of Christ that is more ethereal and situational, while others are committed to Jesus as the way, the truth, and the life. In other words, for some he is *one* option for salvation while for others he is *the* option. That distinction matters, because both things cannot be equally true. Either he is Christ for the whole world, or he is Christ for none of it.

That doesn't mean we have answers for every theological intricacy related to a global gospel. It simply means we believe with Paul that "if you declare with your mouth 'Jesus is Lord,' and believe in your heart that God raised him from the dead, you will be saved" (Romans 10:9).

This—and nothing less than this—is what is being debated in our denomination. Do not be lulled into believing that if we will only learn to "live and let live" on matters of sexuality, then we will all get along otherwise. That simply isn't the case. This debate is over the much more fundamental issue of how the person and work of Jesus is interpreted in the world.

What Faith Is Not

Faith is the life of Christ living itself out in me; it is not passively waiting for things to change without my having to do anything. Read that again: Faith is the life of Christ living itself out in me; it is not passively waiting for things to change without my having to do anything. This idea that things will somehow "all work out" without our having to make fundamental shifts in how we've been doing "church" for the last fifty years is precisely the lie that got The United Methodist Church into the pickle it is currently in. Even now, we hear a collective gasp at the notion that we might end up being different on the other side of this than we are right now. This gasp is not only irrational; it is also anti-Kingdom. The kingdom of God is dynamic, and when God moves we are called to move with him. Friends, we not only *will* end up being different on the other side of this divide. We *should* end up being different. We should be more faithful, more bold, more brave, more hungry for the things of God. We should resist every urge to preserve the institution while we fall headlong into the advancement of the Christian movement.

In fact, the Bible defines faith as movement. James taught that faith without works is dead. Faith for a United Methodist is lived out at the intersection of personal holiness (defined as spiritual discipline) and social holiness (defined as transformational community). We are shaped for this work of letting Christ shape us as we shape our community. As we transform it. Some will wonder how orthodoxy fits together with a call to movement and transformation. I believe it happens as we keep our eyes on Jesus, who calls us to cling not to the form of religion but to the spirit of it.

Tweaking or Transformation

When something important is looming in our lives, we often have a tendency to avoid it by focusing on smaller, less important things. We spend time fine-tuning or tweaking things that are comparatively inconsequential, but we ignore the one thing that really matters. Tweaking the small stuff can make us feel like we've been busy and accomplished a lot, despite knowing that the big stuff isn't being dealt with. My house never gets so clean as when I have a writing project to finish. Maybe you can relate.

It makes me think of the Samaritan woman Jesus met at the well, the one who tried to press him into a discussion about where real worship happens.

"On this mountain or that one?" she asked, to which he replied (in effect), "I'm not sure it matters for you. Until you deal with the fact that you've been married five times and are living with a guy now, what does it matter where worship happens?"

That was another of those days Jesus answered a question with a question.

Or what about those religious leaders who came to Jesus upset because his friends didn't properly wash their hands according to custom before eating? To them, Jesus responded (in spirit), "Good point, actually. And here's an even better one: why don't you take care of your own parents, rather than obsessively letting the rules steal all your compassion and sense of responsibility?"

I can hear Jesus asking me that question when I get all tangled up in some detail or another, and I can also hear him asking our denomination a similar question. "Until you have dealt with what you believe about Jesus, what do these lesser debates accomplish?" In other words, until you have faith in Christ, everything else is tweaking the small stuff. If we fail to deal corporately and authoritatively with this central and supreme issue, we will miss the big moves of God.

Have you faith in Christ? Because your answer to that question matters long before you answer any others.

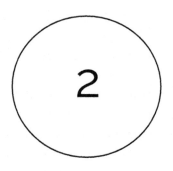

ARE YOU GOING ON TO PERFECTION?

In the span of one question, Wesley delivers us from justification into the deep end of sanctification's waters. A call to Christian perfection is a call to die to self, but it is also an invitation to freedom—freedom from mediocrity and the tyranny of "tolerable." It is an invitation into the good life in its most vivid and faithful form. United Methodists believe Christian perfection (or entire sanctification) is the trajectory of authentic discipleship. Wesley's second question is not whether we have reached it or even if we can. The question is: Are our lives pointed in that direction?

Perfection is a radical expectation. It sounds arrogant, even, but Wesley didn't mean perfection in the sense of being perfect at everything. Perfection in Kingdom terms is not getting all the right answers, having all the right behaviors, never making a mistake, always being on time, and never offending anyone. Far from it! Kingdom perfection has to do with the state of one's heart. It is what Paul said to the Corinthians: "If I speak in the tongues of men or of angels, but do not have love, I am only a resounding gong or a clanging cymbal" (1 Corinthians 13:1). Or consider the words of Micah 6:8: "He has shown you, O mortal, what is good. And what does the LORD require of you? To act justly and to love mercy and to walk humbly with your God."

This is the kind of perfection God craves for us: being made perfect *in love*. This call to Christian perfection is a cry to be something more, but not in the sense of striving for "a better you." This is a call to go with God, to continually seek a deeper, richer, more abundant life in Christ by the power of the Holy Spirit. What we seek as Christians is wholeness, and we believe wholeness is possible because Jesus has power to make all things new.

This call to something new is the goal of sanctification, which is the unique gift of our Wesleyan tradition to the body of Christ. Sanctification is about allowing the Holy Spirit to lead as he flows through us, sending us toward perfect love, perfect joy, perfect peace. Christian perfection is not only attainable, it is the rightful inheritance of those who claim Christ as Lord.

Long before I became a pastor, I had a conversation with a woman who had just been ordained into The United Methodist Church after initially being ordained in another denomination. The conversion was for her a great gift on almost every level. She told me with some surprise, however, that she hadn't expected to answer this question at her ordination. "Did you realize," she asked me incredulously, "that they want to know if you're going on to perfection?" When I asked how she responded to that question, she answered quietly, "Well, I crossed my fingers behind my back and said yes" (betraying, of course, any hint of an idea she might actually be going on to perfection). I don't think Wesley was looking for leaders who were comfortable crossing their fingers . . . *ever*. Wesley not only wanted to know that those preaching the good news about Jesus were heeding the words of Jesus himself ("Be perfect, therefore, as your heavenly Father is perfect" [Matthew 5:48]), he wanted to know they were earnestly seeking after the kind of holy love that comes from a holy God.

I am concerned for those who internally cross their fingers even now as they answer these questions, unable or unwilling to honestly admit where they are on the spiritual spectrum. I say this as one grieved, not just for the denomination that must then host pastors who enter into a covenant dishonestly, but especially for the people who have so missed the mark of sanctification that they will compromise their own integrity for the sake of getting into the system. The stories are legion of pastors quietly assenting to these questions when they have no intention of honoring our doctrines and polity. As an example, one friend shared the story of a seminary student who couldn't make peace with United Methodist doctrine, but said she would lie in order to get herself ordained so she could work for change on the inside. In other words, she would cross her fingers and begin a covenantal relationship on that foundation. I believe Wesley would encourage anyone honestly struggling with a Wesleyan approach to faith to remain committed to that struggle. But remember that the soul of these questions is wholeheartedness, and finger-crossing is not a whole-hearted gesture.

It becomes easier and easier in this social climate, however, to embrace dishonesty for the sake of fulfilling our own agenda. In subtle and not so subtle ways, we are being conditioned for it by the culture at large. Consider how the Internet is configured. The Internet works on algorithms. It tracks what I like and then gives me more of the things for which I already have an affinity. If I go searching online for a certain pair of shoes, for instance, I will notice immediately that I get a lot more ads in the sidebar for shoes like the ones I looked for. This means most of the time when I surf online, I will be presented with things that fit what I already like.

And then there is "google-knowing." Google-knowing is that ability to ask a complex question—like the physics of how a particle can be in two places at the same time—and get the answer in a matter of seconds. I can then repeat that answer even if I understand almost nothing of the substance behind what I'm saying.

This business of producing easy information that molds to our preferences can mess with our relationship with God. Think about the implications. If most of what is presented to us agrees with what we already like, and if all our answers come quickly, then it is hard to want something different than that from God. But what if God wants to tell us something we don't like, not because God is mean but because God is not in the business of working off our preferences? What if God wants to show us the pathway to holiness? What if God wants to set us in the direction of Christian perfection, but we're not interested because that doesn't mold to our preferences or come quickly enough?

What if God wants to call The United Methodist Church to account for drifting from orthodoxy, even if orthodoxy no longer squares with cultural norms or is convenient? What if God is asking us to be peculiar people in a perverse generation? What if our decisions as a denomination result in very difficult changes that don't come easily or feel comfortable?

I've had folks tell me they've heard God tell them to do things that have no basis in what I know of the Bible. I've also learned from my own mistakes that confirmation bias—my own internal fake news system—can keep me from accepting God's truth. Going on toward perfection will lead us past the place where we assign every good thought to God and toward the place where we understand that a genuine encounter with God will be stunning, humbling, transformational and good . . . even if it is uncomfortable.

Remember David, the warrior of the Old Testament who is called "a man after God's own heart." He was a mess of a human being. He committed adultery with his neighbor's wife, then killed the neighbor to cover it up. Somehow he managed to fight past what he must surely have known to be wrong, so he could take this woman as his wife and have children with her.

Nathan, the Israelite prophet, heard about this and confronted David with his sin. He did it by telling David a story about a poor man who owned a lamb that he treasured. The poor man raised that little lamb almost like a child. Then one day a rich man came and took that poor man's lamb to make a meal out of it. As David heard Nathan share the story, he was moved to a kind of righteous anger. He said that any man who did such a thing should be killed. To which Nathan replied, "You're that man."

Coming face to face with his own depravity, his own fallenness, "David said to Nathan, 'I have sinned against the LORD.' And Nathan said to David, 'The LORD also has put away your sin; you shall not die. Nevertheless, because by this deed you have utterly scorned the LORD, the child who is born to you shall die'" (2 Samuel 12:13-14 ESV).

We get the whole experience of repentance in these words: David's genuine remorse, God's genuine forgiveness, the reality that our sins have consequences. We learn that God's kindness toward us is not permission to do as we please. It is permission to be honest without fear of condemnation. No finger-crossing. We discover that God's work is to "holy-fy" us, and that his wrath—God's unchanging position toward sin—ends up being good news. It teaches us that we can depend on God not to change the rules in the middle of the game. Even while he asks us not to cross our fingers, God will not cross his fingers and tell us only what we want to hear.

Finger-crossing is our all-too-human preference for changing the rules rather than changing our hearts. But this work of becoming holy—sanctified—is absolutely a matter of the heart, and it begins with God, not us. So David, the adulterer and murderer, prayed: "Create in me a pure heart, O God, and renew a steadfast spirit within me. Do not cast me from your presence or take your Holy Spirit from me. Restore to me the joy of your salvation and grant me a willing spirit, to sustain me" (Psalm 51:10-12).

This is the prayer of one going on to perfection. This is where holiness begins. It begins in the heart. Whether you are preparing for vocational ministry or just trying to follow Jesus in your work as a banker, I cannot stress enough the importance of setting the trajectory of your life and work toward Christian perfection. Whether you reach that high and lofty goal is not the point. I'm not even concerned with whether you think it is possible. What matters is where you are headed.

Is it your intention to keep on seeking until there is nothing left but Christ alone?

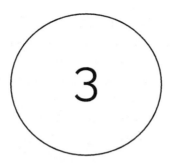

DO YOU EXPECT TO BE MADE PERFECT IN LOVE IN THIS LIFE?

I can almost hear the tone in Wesley's voice as he dictates this question. Having just asked about perfection, now he wants to know if we really mean this. *Seriously, are you going someplace spiritually? Do you actually expect to get there? Or are you just along for the ride?* I can hear his insistence on us taking a long, hard look at what perfection really means and what it will cost. Do we understand this spiritual journey as an active and ongoing pursuit of ever-deepening love? Is this our intention—to be so ruthlessly opposed to stagnation in our life with Christ that we continually press on toward the prize of perfect love?

This, Wesley would say, is the goal. In fact, he claimed full sanctification as the unique contribution of Methodism to the body of Christ: "This doctrine is the grand depositum which God has lodged with the people called Methodists; and for the sake of propagating this chiefly God appeared to have raised us up."[1] Wesley believed Methodists were given to this call, to raise up a people dedicated to taking faith to the radical edge.

Salvation is not fire insurance. It is a bold first step in a lifetime journey of dying to self and living for Christ. This commitment to entire sanctification is ultimately a call to defeat the spirit of fear so that true love might flourish in us, and that is not something that can happen with our spare change or in our spare time. It is an active participation in what the Holy Spirit is doing within us.

To be made perfect in love is to be committed to becoming bolder, more loving, more vulnerable, more courageous in our approach to relationships. This is a heart-level transformation, a journey from shame to acceptance and the standard for those who follow Jesus. It is a lifestyle so saturated in love that it has lost its capacity to be controlled by fear or shame. John makes it plain: "There is no fear in love. But perfect love drives out fear, because fear has to do with punishment. The one who fears is not made perfect in love" (1 John 4:18). The perfection we are after is not behavioral. It is the pursuit of a better brand of love—loving people past our pain and their problems.

Of course, everything that looks like love and walks like love isn't necessarily God's brand of love. Wesley distinguished our brand as "holy love," the kind that transforms us into something different: more humble, more caring, less internally divided. We're just different.

It is like the difference between the generic brand of perfume and the real thing. The bottle may look the same and the packaging may promise that all the same ingredients are used. But if you really know your perfume, you'll be able to smell an off-brand from across the room. It is the same with love. Before we accepted Christ into our lives, we may have been using a generic form of love. When relationships don't heal and rejection reigns, we can assume we have settled for a cheaper version of the real thing. When selfishness is the operative motive, we can be sure of it.

God's brand of love is other-focused. It turns out that only the Holy Spirit can create that kind of love in a person. I would argue, in fact, that the mark of the Holy Spirit is a supernatural ability to love. To put it another way, the only way we can know we have God's brand of love is by receiving God's Spirit into our lives. Likewise, we will know we are filled with the Holy Spirit when we display the kind of unusual love that only God can inspire us to show. As we often say in my church, this is about hanging on to people way past good sense. It is a compulsion to share sacrificially for the sake of another person's joy, not in codependent ways but because we are no longer the center of our attention. This is what it means to be fruitful. It is the cultivation of a kind of lavish and other-focused love that overflows in practical acts of witness and compassion.

Simply put, the Holy Spirit compels me to love even the hard-to-love ones. Maybe especially them.

Love as a concept has been batted about a good bit in recent years. We've heard that love prevails and love wins, and the doctrinal debates have been set up to look as if one side loves while the other side does not. Of course, that isn't true, and it is a shame to see such a central term of the faith used for political ends in this way. But if we are messy and ill-informed in our understanding of love, we are in good company. Think about Paul's first letter to the Corinthian church. Chapter thirteen of that letter contains the most beautiful and sensitive poem on love in the Bible. It is the passage we hear at almost every wedding, though Paul didn't send this letter to folks who were in love with each other. He sent it to one of the most divided, dysfunctional churches of the first century. (The Corinthians make me feel better about my own dysfunction.)

The Corinthians were arguing about food that had been sacrificed to pagan gods, then going off to a church service where they yelled and tried to one-up each other on spiritual gifts. The men were shirking their responsibilities and the women were speaking in tongues right in the middle of the assembly. When Paul started in on them about how to love one another, he was talking to a roomful of folks who were at each other's throats. He wanted them to understand that if love was the defining character trait of a Christian, they would need a new definition of love.

When I talk about the situation with the Corinthians during a wedding, I usually tell the sweet couple standing in front of me that just because this passage was not written for lovers does not necessarily mean it isn't appropriate for such a time as this. We who have been married for any length of time understand that marital love is not a Hallmark card. It is standing with someone as they let go of an unhealthy habit, having patience with the differences that make living together a challenge, loving each other past the pain and brokenness. Most of our opportunities to show authentic love happen in the middle of the stuff of life. No wonder Paul began his poem on love with this line: Love is patient (1 Corinthians 13:4).

For Christians this is a crucial point. God has called us to love him and love others not just when we feel like it or when it is easy or when the other person is lovable, but all the time, and especially when it is hard. We are called to love the Samaritans, the folks who are not socially acceptable and fun to be around. This is not a call to agreement on issues. This is call to care for souls even as we follow Jesus. We are never given permission to devalue others or send them to hell, even in our minds. That job does not belong to us. We are called to go beyond tolerance in order to love as Jesus loved, and even to aspire to love perfectly from a pure heart.

Even the hard-to-love ones. Maybe especially them.

Do you remember the day Jesus stood up in the temple and read from the Holy Scriptures? The scene is painted in Luke 4, and Jesus was reading from Isaiah 61: "The Spirit of the Lord is upon me, because he has anointed me to bring good news to the poor. He has sent me to proclaim release to the captives and recovery of sight to the blind, to let the oppressed go free, to proclaim the year of the Lord's favor" (Luke 4:18-19 NRSV). After he rolled up the scroll and gave it back to the priest, he proceeded to go out and do the very things he has given to us to do—to love the poor, the oppressed, the prisoners, the blind, those who never knew they had God's favor.

Nowhere in this definition of Kingdom love does Jesus mention emotion. This is an important point. Perfect love is not a feeling; it is a lifestyle, an obedience. God isn't consigning us to a perpetual group hug. I can tell you, you won't last long among the poor, the prisoners, the disabled, the oppressed, if you are faking it. That has been a hard lesson in my own life and ministry. I want to look like Mother Teresa, but the fact is that I get frustrated with people. I get angry and impatient and offended. On my own steam, I'm not very loving. The kind of love Jesus prescribes can only happen under the influence and power of the Holy Spirit.

If we have any hope at all of perfecting our capacity for love—of being made perfect in this life—we must pursue a baptism in the Holy Spirit that drenches us in the very power of God, which, as it turns out, is love. Otherwise, as Paul says, it is all a charade. If your business is going great and everything you touch turns to hundred-dollar bills, but your relationships are going down the toilet, then you are missing the point of living the Christian life as Jesus called you to live it. If your ministry is increasing in numbers and all the bills are being paid, but in your ambitious pursuits you have lost your love for your family at home, then you are missing the whole point. If you are doctrinally sound and can quote all the verses to prove your point but you have no patience for those who disagree, then all that knowledge is for nothing. It will not last.

As for blogs and position papers, they will not matter in a hundred years. As for big gatherings and bold proclamations, they will pass away. Probably no one will be talking about your great sermon or your great program or your snappiest tweet when you die. They will talk about how well you loved God and other people. This is the essence, Wesley wrote, of real religion:

> And this we conceive to be no other than love; the love of God and of all mankind; the loving God with all our heart, and soul, and strength, as having first loved us, as the fountain of all the good we have received, and of all we ever hope to enjoy; and the loving every soul which God hath made, every man on earth, as our own soul.

> This love we believe to be the medicine of life, the never failing remedy for all the evils of a disordered world, for all the miseries and vices of men. . . .

> This religion we long to see established in the world, a religion of love, and joy, and peace, having its seat in the heart, in the inmost soul, but ever showing itself by its fruits, continually springing forth."[2]

Oswald Chambers says, "Sanctification is an impartation, not an imitation."[3] The whole work of sanctification is the transformation of lives for the transformation of the world. The Spirit takes control of our minds and purifies our thoughts. We need this. We need the Holy Spirit to invade us in the hidden space of our souls, so we can be taught there how to love people.

Hear this question as a call (and a requirement, if you are a pastor) to be filled with the Holy Spirit, because it is only through the power of the Holy Spirit that you will be able to love as Jesus loves.

---

1 John Wesley, Letter to Robert Carr Brackenbury, September 15th, 1790. http://wesley .nnu.edu/john-wesley/the-letters-of-john-wesley/wesleys-letters-1790b/

2 John Wesley, "An Earnest Appeal to Men of Reason and Religion," in *The Works of the Reverend John Wesley, Sometime Fellow of Lincoln College, Oxford*, First American Complete and Standard Edition, vol. 5 (New York: B. Waugh and T. Mason 1835), 5.

3 Oswald Chambers, "Sanctification (2)," July 23, *My Utmost for His Highest*, first published in the United States in 1934. Available at https://utmost.org/sanctification-2/.

ARE YOU EARNESTLY STRIVING AFTER IT?

In my growing-up years, my family lived on a dirt road in a working-class neighborhood. The driveways were dirt, the houses were basic, and most folks on my block had a garden in the backyard, not for fun but for food. Given that setting, it was unusual that my dad would build a concrete basketball court on our property. It wasn't a full-sized court, but it was big enough for a pick-up game and the hoop was regulation height. A concrete court made our backyard a popular place with the neighborhood kids.

I was too young to get invited into the serious games among my four brothers, but I loved playing "horse" and "pig" on that court. I still love the sound of a dribbling ball. It sounds like Saturday to me. Like home. I learned a few things about life on that court. I learned that taking a shot—even a sloppy one—is more gratifying than having the ball stolen by a boy. I learned that when people make fun of your knobby knees to get you off your game, you have two choices: tell Mom or make a shot that makes them forget you're a scrawny little girl. I also learned a lot of grace from my dad, who was always willing to let me take a "do-over" when I missed the basket by a mile.

I learned from that court that if you want to get good at something, you have to practice. Good form doesn't just happen. It starts with hundreds of messy shots. You have to figure out how a ball moves across your hand, how to jump and throw, when to release. Basketball is a fast-moving sport that takes a lot of concentration. Finding your own style, stride, and strategy is what separates the backyard dribblers from the serious players.

When Kobe Bryant retired, he was the third-highest scoring player of all time, and he got there using a style completely unique to him. When making shots, Kobe tended to release the ball at the top of his jump. In other words, the ball didn't leave his hand until he was as high in the air as he could get. This isn't how anyone else does it. For 99.9 percent of us, the most consistent way to score in basketball is not to shoot while hanging in the air at the top of a jump, but to release the ball on the way up.

No one else in pro ball did that like Kobe, but somehow he figured out this unique style and it not only set him apart, but made him a champion. As a consequence, teenagers everywhere who dreamed of being the next Kobe Bryant tried in vain to mimic that style, waiting until the top of their jump to release the ball. The result was a lot of frustrated kids missing a lot of baskets when what they really needed was someone to encourage them to find their own style.

What is true in basketball is true in life. Most of us need to find our own style and be at peace with letting go before we get to the top of our jump. We don't want to hear this because most of us want to control everything before we surrender any of it. "I'll learn to love these people when they all behave as I would like." "I'll quit my habit when I get past this rough spot." "I'll start leaning into my devotional life when I'm past these deadlines." "I'll start praying when I get my life together or when I get past this busy stretch." We think we have to wait until we are at the top of our jump to make the shot, but that strategy only leads to frustration. Rather than waiting until all the details are lined up, all the questions answered, all the crises averted, the best place to "release the ball" is *before* you have everything under your control. Otherwise, what is faith for? Or grace? Or surrender?

I believe this is the spirit of Wesley's fourth question: release control and trust the process. The best way to go after Christian perfection is to make room for hundreds of messy shots, thousands of mistakes, and countless do-overs on the way to figuring out your own style, strengths, and strategy.

"Earnestly striving" sounds a little intimidating, doesn't it? With the right tone of voice, that phrase conjures up visions of angry coaches yelling at kids to try harder. We know this isn't the case, though, because ours is a gospel of grace. We are not being asked here to channel our inner perfectionist. Instead, take this question as permission to keep trying, even if for a while (maybe even a lifetime) it is going to look messy and we'll miss a lot of shots and need a lot of do-overs. This question is permission to release the ball on the way up, rather than waiting until we are at the top of our jump. It is also a reminder—again—that we won't reach Christian perfection in our spare time using only our spare change. That word *earnestly* implies both intentionality and sacrifice. It implies single-mindedness and whole-heartedness. Christian perfection is not a hobby; it is a lifestyle.

I was called by God into vocational ministry when I was thirteen years old. Back then, it was a rare thing to see a woman in church leadership. Without strong role models or good teaching to back up the call, I struggled to make it work. By the time I got to college, I had watered down my call. Rather than being a pastor, I would be a director of Christian education. My pastor said that would be a better fit. He might have been right, except that I am a disaster in a roomful of children. I love kids, but children's ministry is not my gift (trust me on this; I tried). It was terribly frustrating trying to "shoot" like another person shoots rather than finding my own style.

As a result, I stepped away from my call at the age of seventeen and when I did, I also stepped away from my faith. I didn't realize how intertwined those two things are. The result was ten disastrous years of wandering in the desert. I met my husband during that dark and faithless season. Neither of us was a practicing Christian at the time, but somehow we ended up on our first date talking about what it takes to become a pastor. I was arguing (I thought, brilliantly) that people who screw up really big in life don't deserve to become pastors once they straighten up. Steve argued (he thought, biblically) that God can use anybody. During the course of that meal, Steve looked right at me and said he thought I would make a great pastor. At the time, I was holding a beer in one hand and a cigarette in the other, so I can only conclude that his experience with pastors was very different from mine.

I couldn't have disagreed more, but then I was still operating out of some faulty mentality that convinced me I could only shoot if I was at the top of my jump. It took about ten years from that first date for me to get it that God does not give as the world gives. God uses all kinds of people—really holy ones and really messed-up ones, funny ones and serious ones, laid-back ones and wound-tight ones. God is perfectly happy to use all kinds of styles, strengths, and strategies to accomplish God's purposes, because (don't miss this point) while God is perfect, God is not a perfectionist.

By asking us to "earnestly strive" after Christian perfection, no one is asking us to get it right the first time or every time or even ever. The wisdom embedded in this question is the wisdom of "the try." It is a call to keep on asking, keep on seeking, keep on knocking, never assuming that our own sanctification or anyone else's is a done deal.

One more bit of basketball trivia: Did you know that if you shoot straight for the basket, you have less chance of making a shot than if you shoot above it? It is all in the arc. They tell me that a shot made at a 35-degree angle— just about exactly the rise needed to reach the basket (recognizing that the height of the player figures into the equation)—has almost no margin of error. In other words, that shot has to be almost perfect to make the score, even more perfect to do so without hitting the rim. But give that shot another 10 degrees (a 45-degree angle) and the margin of error increases exponentially. Just by shooting a little higher, your chances of making the shot— even if your form is messy, your jump is off, and the ball wobbles on the way up—increase exponentially.

Maybe this is the warning beneath this question: don't shoot too low. Worry less about form and more about the heart beneath your next shot. Isn't this just what Paul taught Timothy? He warned that there would be those so concerned with money, pleasure, and self-gratification that they would miss God in the bargain, "having a form of godliness but denying its power" (2 Timothy 3:5). Paul warned against the kind of behavior-management and trouble-shooting that gets so caught up in getting everything "right" that we miss out on righteousness. Instead of shooting for transformation, we shoot for something less.

Are you shooting too low? Are you so caught up in the details that you're missing the big picture? Are you trying too hard to copy someone else's form rather than practicing your own? Be encouraged. God is perfect, but he is not a perfectionist. Learn the voice of grace. Keep practicing your own spiritual style, recognizing that good form doesn't just happen. It starts with hundreds of messy shots.

Go after your own sanctification and your own healing with your whole heart. This is all you have to offer anyone. All the talent in the world is useless if you don't have a hunger for holiness.

5

ARE YOU RESOLVED TO DEVOTE YOURSELF WHOLLY TO GOD AND GOD'S WORK?

Most anyone who has ever held a part-time position in a church will be the first to tell you there is really no such thing as "part-time" in church work. "Part-time" is a carrot they dangle so they can get you on the payroll and soak up every minute of you, but maybe that isn't such a bad thing. As I have said several times before, this work is not meant to be carried out with our leftover time or leftover money. Jesus never gave us that option. He calls those who follow earnestly to take up crosses, die to self, leave it all on the table. We are even told that those who preach and teach are held to a higher standard. "Not many of you should become teachers, my fellow believers," James warns, "because you know that we who teach will be judged more strictly" (James 3:1).

If the only option open to us is wholeheartedness—being wholly devoted to God and his work—then how do we know we have it? What is the litmus test for wholeheartedness? What spiritual work must we tackle before we can give ourselves completely to this vocation of serving Jesus? We know from both Scripture and experience that it isn't our skill set that gets us there, nor is it our awesome connections or superior ability to do everything just right. This business of wholeheartedness is a spiritual operation. It is what it says it is: heart-level wholeness.

What does it mean to become whole, by biblical standards? Surely it begins with Paul's advice to work out your own salvation daily with fear and trembling. Stay in it, Paul advises, and wrestle with what it looks like in your life. Let the daily wrestling expose the cracks and wounds. Deal with the unholy fears that paralyze you, leaving you stranded out there in the desert, unable to make the journey into the promises of God. Acknowledge your doubts, and dare to believe God can handle them. To become wholehearted, we must deal with our wounds and hesitations, fears and doubts, even as we develop eyes to see what God sees.

When I was a little girl, I often had nightmares. I'd wake up petrified and run for my parents' room. I wanted my mother's comfort. But it was dark, and things in the dark look ominous. If there was anything on the floor of their bedroom—clothes, bedroom shoes, anything that could be misinterpreted in the dark—I'd end up standing paralyzed in the doorway, just feet from their bed, unable to reach my mom for fear of what that thing on the floor might be. I always assumed the worst.

Carry the remnants of those early fears into adulthood and they begin to look remarkably familiar to many of us. We allow all kinds of things to generate fear within, to stand between us and the comfort we so desperately need. We become afraid of getting too close to others, afraid of losing control, afraid of going too far with God, maybe even afraid of succeeding (too much pressure!). We can become paralyzed by irrational fears. The writer of Leviticus has our number. He describes a conversation between God and his people. If the Israelites continue to disobey, their land will be devastated and the people will be scattered. "And for those of you who survive, I will demoralize you in the land of your enemies. You will live in such fear that the sound of a leaf driven by the wind will send you fleeing. You will run as though fleeing from a sword, and you will fall even when no one pursues you. Though no one is chasing you, you will stumble over each other as though fleeing from a sword. You will have no power to stand up against your enemies" (Leviticus 26:36-37 NLT).

Paralyzing fear takes away our power to fight the enemy. We become reactionary and prone toward survival-level decisions. Fear makes for terrible career choices. What spiritual work do you need to do in order to admit to and deal with the irrational and self-limiting fears in your life? Are you resolved to do that healing work? *Resolved* does not mean "only if it gets out of control" or "until something better comes along." Resolved means surrendered, submitted, committed, sacrificially obedient. Being resolved to devote myself wholly to God means going after wholeness in my life, no matter the cost.

Too much of our conversation in The UMC is driven by fear. For decades, fear has kept us from talking lovingly and honestly about our differences. Fear is keeping congregations from frank discussions about our current crisis. Fear has kept us in a defensive crouch. Fear has kept us from acknowledging the depth of our divide. We have wanted to characterize it as a simple paper cut when it is in fact a gaping wound breeding infection. By minimizing the differences, we may stifle a crisis that is actually our opportunity—if we're bold enough to accept change as a good thing—to give clearly unique theological positions a chance to live with more integrity and to prove themselves by their fruit.

I hear echoes of angels in this moment before us, encouraging, "Be not afraid." Meanwhile, we shrink back, for fear of what we might lose if we act boldly.

Fear is the great enemy of wholeheartedness.

Two years after the Israelites were delivered from their five hundred years of oppressive slavery in Egypt, they found themselves standing on the brink of the land God promised them. To get to this place, they had seen waters part and enemies drown. Yahweh was intimately involved with their lives. They knew him. They followed him. And just two short years after packing up and moving out of bondage, there they stood on the brink of God's best. Yes, there were vicious armies and untamed wilds on the other side of that border, but they had the smoke and fire of God blazing their trail.

Then it happened. Human nature kicked in.

They became more cautious than optimistic. There at the edge of God's plan, they sent a dozen spies into that question mark of a promise to check things out. Ten returning spies slinked back with a warning: "Don't do it! It is great real estate, but the people are giants. We will all die if we go over there." The majority report was full of fear and trepidation.

The other two spies—young men named Joshua and Caleb—looked on that land and saw a future with hope. For them, the land was more possibility than problems. "I think we should do this," they challenged. "This is God's land and God's fight. Let God defend us!"

The people did what people mostly do. They allowed the voice of fear to drown out the voice of potential and it cost them dearly.

That day, God turned them back from the border of promise. He sent them out into the wilderness again where he promptly vowed that not one of their generation would see the land flowing with milk and honey. Fear would not be woven into the DNA of his chosen people, not if God had anything to do with it.

So the people got in the wilderness what they were most afraid of getting in the promised land. They were destroyed by their own choice. For thirty-eight years they wandered like dead men walking before another generation found itself toe-to-toe with God's purposes.

I wonder if most of that first generation even knew how close they were to greatness? I wonder if, way down the road, some of them sat around campfires and wondered aloud, "What do you suppose would have become of us if we had listened to Joshua and Caleb? How do you suppose it would have turned out?" Did they even stop to think about it as they poked their fires or packed up their tents yet again or held their cups beneath water flowing from rocks?

Did they think that deeply? Did they assume, like most people, that what they had twenty or thirty years out from that decision was all there was? Did they ever stop to imagine more than mediocrity punctuated by death? Or did they simply go about their lives, making grocery lists, making beds, making a living, making do?

I wonder, but I can't judge. After all, I am an Israelite myself. I peek over into spiritual promises and my little internal band of spies reports back, "That'll never work for you," and far too often I listen to those voices of fear or laziness or institutional caution and I miss out. Who knows how long I've wandered, unaware of the promises I've turned down, while God in his mercy determines to kill off all in me that reeks of fear?

Who knows how long our denomination as a whole will wander, while God in his mercy determines to kill off all in us that reeks of fear? What if, even now, we are wandering in a desert of our own making, unable to imagine more than mediocrity punctuated by death? Friends, fear is a killer. It kills spirits and can even thwart great moves of God. I hope we are not hanging on to an institution simply because we are afraid of stepping into God's vision for us.

Are you resolved to devote yourself *wholly*? Not half-heartedly. Not with your spare change and spare time. Not only as far as your comforts will take you. Not fearfully, but wholly to God and God's work? In your study and worship and fellowship and serving and in the truth you share, be passionately committed to the pursuit of wholeness so you can be in passionate pursuit of the presence of Christ. Without that kind of vulnerable, wholehearted faith, it is impossible to please God.

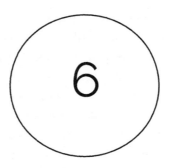

6

DO YOU KNOW THE GENERAL RULES OF OUR CHURCH?

Psychologist Susan Pinker has presented a TED talk about the residents of a tiny island called Sardinia, off the coast of Italy. What distinguishes the citizens of Sardinia is their unusual ability to live beyond one hundred years. The island has six times more centenarians than the mainland and ten times more than North America. The phenomenon has attracted the attention of researchers and after significant study, they've come to this conclusion: more than exercise, healthy eating habits, the lack of unhealthy habits like smoking or drinking, Sardinians live longer because of their commitment to social interaction. Face-to-face interaction releases all kinds of positive chemicals in our bodies that bolster our immune systems. Pinker says, "It is a biological imperative to know we belong."[1]

Science has proven what the Bible has already told us: we need each other. It is how we are made. We are designed to follow Jesus within the care of community.

First-century followers of Jesus understood the critical importance of sharing in each other's lives. They met together, sharing in meals, study, and prayer (Acts 2:42). This profound equation for community came to define the early church. So much more than a worship service, the early church was a lifestyle.

As Methodism caught fire across the early American landscape, John Wesley wisely applied the same equation to its first adherents. By instituting class meetings as a core value in the movement, Wesley found the secret to the enduring success of this movement.

> It can scarce be conceived what advantages have been reaped from this little prudential regulation. Many now happily experienced that Christian fellowship of which they had not so much as an idea before. They began to "bear one another's burdens," and "naturally" to "care for each other." As they had daily a more intimate acquaintance with, so they had a more endeared affection for each other. And "speaking the truth in love, they grew up into Him in all things which is the head, even Christ; from whom the whole body, fitly joined together, and compacted by that which every joint supplied, according to the effectual working in the measure of every part, increased unto the edifying itself in love."[2]

Those early meetings weren't about information. They were about transformation. United Methodist scholar Kevin Watson writes, "Early Methodists were asked to invite others into their lives and to be willing to enter deeply into the lives of other people so that together they would grow in grace. They were committed to the idea that the Christian life is a journey of growth in grace, or sanctification. And they believed that they needed one another in order to persevere on this journey."[3] These early-generation Methodists looked across the world at the state of the body of Christ and concluded that community was essential.

To grow together in healthy community, Wesley prescribed three very general rules: Do no harm. Do good. Observe the ordinances of God. These were meant to foster healthy, committed relationships among followers of Jesus, to strengthen the fabric of a community. To understand and appreciate these rules is to commit to the values of the kingdom of God.

Do No Harm

This seems on the surface like an unnecessary word. Surely, grown adults don't have to be told to not harm each other . . . right? Except that we do it all the time. Not in obvious ways, of course. Most of us don't kill people or do boldly illegal things. We don't play around with evil on purpose, and we try to stay on the right side of the Ten Commandments. We know how to avoid the more conspicuous harmful things. But it turns out that some of the worst damage is inflicted not by the obvious things but by more subtle forms of unkindness. Greed causes Christians to do harm by making us stingy when we ought to be generous. Fear causes us to be unkind by fostering a lack of trust. Living an undisciplined life can wreak havoc on all our relationships. When we can't follow through on commitments because we've over-committed, and when we don't honor others' time because we're disorganized and unprepared, we frazzle other people and fray our relationships around the edges.

Think honestly about this. Do you use people for your own ambitious ends? Do you stretch yourself to your emotional limits, so that others have to contend with your mood swings? Do you tend to the state of your heart not just for your own sake, but for the sake of doing no harm to others?

Be clear on this: doing no harm does not mean "never disagree." To the contrary, I would say that sometimes a refusal to call someone out on their foolishness is the most harmful thing you can do to them, not to mention plain unkind. Who wants to be left to sit in their sin while others use politeness to avoid confrontation?

In the issues being debated in The UMC these days, there is a premium placed on tolerance. Yet, our core value as Christians is not tolerance but holiness. God commanded that we are to be holy, because the Lord God is holy (Leviticus 20:26, 1 Peter 1:16). Holiness informs my response to the culture around me. My opinions must be rooted in the values of holiness as I find them in the Bible. I don't interpret the Bible in light of how the world turns. I interpret the world in light of the Bible, even when it means I will look a little crazy by the world's standards.

Holiness does not give me a pass on practicing a whole host of other character-defining traits, such as patience, humility, gentleness, endurance, bearing with one another in love. When followers of Jesus take this call to holiness seriously then eventually they will look less like the world and more like the kingdom of heaven in the ways they live life. I pray like crazy that as I live the art of holiness, I will "do no harm," as Wesley counseled.

If you want to know what it means to "do no harm," follow the thread of "one anothers" through the New Testament and you'll discover your answer. First-century followers of Jesus devoted themselves to fellowship, tending to the "one anothers" prescribed by the Bible—not grumbling among one another (John 6:43), not biting at one another (Galatians 5:15), not envying one another (Galatians 5:26), not complaining against one another (James 4:11), bearing with and forgiving one another (Colossians 3:13). The shortest path from doing no harm to doing good is other-focused living.

Do Good

If doing no harm is the "being" side of community-building, then doing good is the "doing" side. Authentic communities of Christ are *doing* communities. James instructs us in this:

> What good is it, dear brothers and sisters, if you say you have faith but don't show it by your actions? Can that kind of faith save anyone? Suppose you see a brother or sister who has no food or clothing, and you say, "Good-bye and have a good day; stay warm and eat well"—but then you don't give that person any food or clothing. What good does that do? So you see, faith by itself isn't enough. Unless it produces good deeds, it is dead and useless.
>
> *(James 2:14-17 NLT)*

It's not that we work our way to heaven, but without works, there is no proof of what we believe. This is our divine design. Our faith is connected to what we do, and what we do connects us to each other.

There is an African story about a rat who lived in a farmer's house. Rat had a great rat life. He did all the good rat things, until one day when he looked through his usual hole in the wall to see Farmer and his wife opening a package. When they got it open and produced the contents, Rat was mortified to see that they had bought a rat trap. He called the animals together and said, "We have to do something! This is terrible. There is a rat trap in the house!" Cow, Goat, and Chicken listened to Rat ranting and raving about this rat trap, then Chicken said, "You know, I never heard of a chicken getting caught in a rat trap. Hmm." And with that, the chicken walked away. Goat was more sympathetic. He said, "Gosh, Rat. This is a terrible turn of events for you. Please be careful. And I want you to know that we'll be praying for you!" Cow, meanwhile, was chewing his cud and thinking, trying to make sense of the whole rat trap thing and its connection to his world. Finally, he looked up at the rat and lazily said, "Well . . . there you have it." And he continued to chew his cud, safe in the knowledge that some things just *are*. So the rat was left alone to deal with his problem.

That night, the rat trap went off. There was a great scream, the lights went on, and the farmer was horrified to see what happened. It seems that a snake, while snapping at the rat who himself was dangerously close to the trap, got caught in the trap. And the farmer's wife, reaching down to get what she thought was a dead rat, got bitten by the snake. The farmer rushed her to the hospital, but sadly she died. The farmer came home, in shock, sick to death over his loss. Well, you know what you need when you are sick, right? Chicken soup. And after the funeral, so many folks came to the house that the farmer prepared beef tips for all of them.

The moral of the story is that we are all connected. Our faith is connected to what we do, and what we do connects us to each other.

You see, when Jesus was nailed to the cross, he nailed us to our neighbor. Living this faith means being concerned for those around us, whoever they are, because we are all connected by the same cross. Jesus said that in the last days, "the King will say to those on his right, 'Come, you who are blessed by my Father, inherit the Kingdom prepared for you from the creation of the world. For I was hungry, and you fed me. I was thirsty, and you gave me a drink. I was a stranger, and you invited me into your home. I was naked, and you gave me clothing. I was sick, and you cared for me. I was in prison, and you visited me'" (Matthew 25:34-36 NLT). Jesus said those who serve like this, from the heart, will be so fully other-focused that they won't even realize what they've done, so he will say to them (v. 40), "I tell you the truth, when you did it to one of the least of these my brothers and sisters, you were doing it to me!"

Observe the Ordinances of God

The ordinances of God are what we might call spiritual disciplines or means of grace, things like public worship, ministry of the Word, the Lord's Supper, family and private prayer, searching the Scriptures, fasting or abstinence, meeting together, and caring for the poor. The means of grace are the things I do that lead me more directly under the influence of the Holy Spirit. This rule, then, is a challenge toward spiritual transformation. It is an inspiration to grow more deeply into holiness.

In the most freeing of ways, Jesus knows us. He hears our hearts. He knows our fierce loves, our anxious thoughts, and our wounded spirits. We are all recovering from instability. Depending on how rebellious we are, we push against holy boundaries. Without discipline, direction, or limits, we only hurt ourselves and others and lose all effectiveness as followers of Jesus. Surely this was Paul's point when he warns us not to run aimlessly (1 Corinthians 9:26).

The ordinances are our antidote to chaotic living. They press us into community and call us to account for making spiritual progress. The key to keeping these practices is in the intention of the user. Spiritual discipline doesn't happen accidentally or coincidentally; it is sought after, like a hungry person looks for food.

When Wesley asks if we know the General Rules, I suspect he is really asking if we have owned them. When we own them, these rules are not really rules at all. They are our ticket to getting a Kingdom perspective and making a Kingdom investment for the sake of a Kingdom impact. It is one thing to know what is right. It is another thing completely to be committed to it. Am I concerned only for my immediate surroundings—*my* family, *my* workplace, *my* church—or do I have the mind-set of a Kingdom Christian? Is my heart yet broken for the whole community of faith? Am I so committed to loving the other that I will hold myself accountable to holy practices that strengthen my own soul and by extension the fabric of the community of Christ?

I wonder how it might change the spiritual atmosphere of your home, your church, your ministry if you began a regular practice of reviewing and observing these rules, making them the centerpiece of your life in Christ and his community?

1 Susan Pinker, "The Secret To Living Longer May Be Your Social Life," TED 2017, https://www.ted.com/talks/susan_pinker_the_secret_to_living_longer_may_be_your _social_life.

2 John Wesley, Letter to Vincent Perronet, December 1748, http://wesley.nnu.edu /john-wesley/the-letters-of-john-wesley/wesleys-letters-1748/.

3 Kevin Watson, Vital Piety, blog entry, July 10, 2010, https://vitalpiety.com/2010/07/30 /the-methodist-class-meeting-for-the-21st-century-the-foundation/.

WILL YOU KEEP THEM?

We have both renters and homeowners living in my neighborhood. I know this, only because every once in a while someone moves out of the house they've been living in and rather than a "for sale" sign popping up in the yard, a "for rent" sign shows up. Since all else is fairly equal, that sign might be the first time I notice that the owners of the home don't live there, and that the residents of that home might not be invested in the future of the neighborhood or value of the property in quite the same way I am.

If they aren't as invested in the same way, I certainly don't blame them. I've been a renter, so I know what it is like to live on that side of the equation. When my husband and I were renters, we knew it wasn't our responsibility to invest in the value of the home. When repairs were needed, we called the owner. When upgrades were considered, we reminded ourselves that we were "strangers in a strange land" and we socked our money away for the day we could own a home of our own.

Ownership changes perspective. It changes the motivation to invest. In the same way that some of us live as renters and some as owners of land and houses, I also suspect that some of us live as renters and some as owners of the core values of Methodism. The General Rules are our values. These three simple rules ought to be the filters through which our doctrines and polity flow as we live them out. To put it plainly, we are to live out our doctrine and polity without doing harm, by doing good, while we are attending to the ordinances of God that lay the foundation for all our work. We live out our polity graciously, without intending to hurt those who disagree. We model the best spirit of our doctrines by taking every opportunity to do good. And we allow the ordinances of God to shape our hearts, so our behavior is not just mimicking goodness but an overflow of it.

In his letter to the Philippians, Paul talks about this process of ownership. On his journey toward complete surrender to the gospel message, he shares how he is moving from renting to owning:

> *Indeed, I count everything as loss because of the surpassing worth of knowing Christ Jesus my Lord. For his sake I have suffered the loss of all things and count them as rubbish, in order that I may gain Christ and be found in him, not having a righteousness of my own that comes from the law, but that which comes through faith in Christ, the righteousness from God that depends on faith— that I may know him and the power of his resurrection, and may share his sufferings, becoming like him in his death, that by any means possible I may attain the resurrection from the dead. Not that I have already obtained this or am already perfect, but I press on to make it my own, because Christ Jesus has made me his own.*
>
> *(Philippians 3:8-12, ESV)*

"I press on to make it my own." Pressing on is an act of hope. Pressing on acknowledges that I may not be who I want to be, but at least I'm not who I was. Pressing on is a commitment to living this life in Christ, day after day, owning it, not just calling in when there is a problem needing repair but investing in what I've been given.

Paul teaches us that in order to press on toward ownership of this Christ-shaped life, we must count everything else as loss. In other words, to take hold and press on, we have to let go. I don't know much about trapeze artistry, but I'm thinking that one of the keys to being a good trapeze artist is knowing when to let go of the trapeze you're leaving before you take hold of the one you're heading toward. I notice when I watch them perform that there is a moment between one trapeze and the next when the artist is truly flying through the air with (what looks like) "the greatest of ease." The artist has let go of one bar but hasn't yet grabbed the other one. This must be the art of it. I suspect one who tries to hold on to both bars at once will end up with a dislocated shoulder or two. Hanging by the two bars at once can't be comfortable. Or safe.

So what happens when I claim the values of Jesus but don't let go of my judgmental anger? Hanging onto those two worlds at once is uncomfortable at best and dangerous at worst. When I call myself a Christian but don't walk in forgiveness, I'm left hanging between two worlds. When I promise I will do no harm, but don't let go of small acts of injustice in my own life that degrade society at large, I'm living dangerously. What happens when I'm called to do good but can't quite let go of selfish ambition? How does it affect my integrity when I refuse to surrender old hurts, a festering anger, and unhealthy habits? How does it read to the rest of the world when I claim Christ but ignore the means of grace while I live an undisciplined life?

This is a place where the Methodist Middle must make choices. There is a danger for those in the middle of hanging between two worlds. There is a misconception that the conservative wing is fixated on preserving the past, but nothing could be further from the truth. The fact is that the past has been institutionalized and even petrified. Conservatives and progressives alike are hungry to move forward. It is which direction forward we're debating. None of us ought to want to somehow float through this crisis without letting go of what is behind. What a waste of a good crisis that would be!

Paul goes on in Philippians 3:13, "One thing I do: Forgetting what is behind and straining toward what is ahead." If I'm going to own these general rules as my own core values, I have to let go of who I used to be and strain toward holiness of heart and life. This kind of spiritual work is not for the faint of heart. It is also not a solitary pursuit. We need folks to hold us accountable, to stay connected to us as we press on, to call us out and also to catch us when we fall. Accountability and connection are fundamental to Methodism, because it is only with accountability and connection that we have any hope of practicing this art of holiness.

Being accountable simply means being responsible for decisions and commitments I make and for actions I take. I am not an island unto myself. I am responsible to God, myself, my circle, and my community for my decisions and actions. I am responsible for upholding the values of the Kingdom of God and for regularly confessing my sins and shortcomings to God and my accountability partners without shame or deceit. Even though I lament it more than I celebrate it, it is a fact that our connection as United Methodists is a strength. As a pastor in this connection, I am not a free agent out there teaching in Jesus' name with no accountability. I'm also not totally responsible for knowing when I'm effective and when I'm not. There are people keeping watch over my ministry who will let me know when it's time to move on without booting me out on the street because the fit isn't right. Those same people are charged with not allowing me to change the rules without consequence.

Confession is important. I'm pretty sure accountability is *not* telling someone in your small group how many times you missed your quiet time this week so they can tell you how many times they missed theirs. Accountability is committing to transformation. After all, Jesus didn't come into his ministry saying, "Talk about your junk and believe, for the kingdom of heaven is near." He said, "*Repent* and believe." Confession isn't the point (it is the start, but not the goal). Change is the point. Accountability is about getting support, so we can let go of what is behind and strain forward toward God's values.

Our General Rules paint those values with a very broad brush. As United Methodists, we are not given permission to be spiteful, selfish, or mean. We are not to be passive in our care of others, either. It is not enough just to avoid hurting anyone. We are called to kindness, patience, compassion. And all these traits must rest not on "shoulds" and "oughts" but on a spiritual foundation of truth and grace. We must own this and help others own it.

This is the heartbeat of integrity. It is to so own the values of the kingdom of God that the world's "normal" is no longer our goal. At its core, a life of integrity isn't behavior management. It is the development of faith in the power of God. Integrity is owning this life in Christ, pressing on, growing up, being accountable to the community of faith, so I don't stay on the same merry-go-round year after year while I complain about how hard it is to change. Integrity is owning my citizenship in heaven and believing that the power available to me is the same power that raises people from the dead. My resources for spiritual transformation are the cattle on a thousand hills, the Messiah of the universe, God and all his angels. My part is to live in this world as if that is so.

Will you keep the General Rules, not just on your wall but in your heart? Will you let them change you? Will you practice them as if you own them? For those of us who want to see the Kingdom come on earth as it is in heaven, how we act is incredibly important. How we act in the midst of conflict is more important still. Others who haven't been on this road as long as we have are watching. How we speak to one another, how we wash each other's feet, how we bear with one another in love and forgive one another as we've been forgiven, how we confess our sins to one another and encourage one another and even greet one another, how we lead one another and, perhaps especially relevant in this season, how we disagree with one another, all this determines the quality of grace we have to offer anyone coming from death to life.

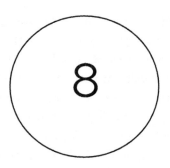

HAVE YOU STUDIED THE DOCTRINES OF THE UNITED METHODIST CHURCH?

There is an old tale about four blind men and an elephant (this is not a politically correct tale, just an old one). As the story goes, each man is stationed around an elephant, the men's experience of the elephant limited by what is within their grasp. The man standing by the leg decides that an elephant must be a kind of tree. The man holding the tail declares it to be a rope. The man who touches the trunk determines the elephant to be a snake. The one by the massive side of the animal concludes that an elephant must be a wall. Each of them interprets his "elephant" solely according to his own limited experience of it. The moral of the story is that none of us has the full range of truth. We each have our corner of it. Our unique perspectives color our understanding of the whole. That is a favorite parable for some universalists, who want us to believe Muslims, Buddhists, Hindus, Jews, and Christians are all equally right and equally limited. Each has a corner of the truth and a unique way of expressing it, but we are gathered around the same God.

And that, brothers and sisters, is just plain bad theology. For starters, it is an insult to every religion. To say all of us are equally right is to ignore the obvious and opposing differences between these religions. No serious Hindu can lay claim to one god exclusive of all others. A faithful Muslim will not embrace the Trinity, and in fact considers that doctrine heretical. Jews are still waiting for their Messiah, while Christians cannot imagine a God apart from Jesus. To say these varied theologies are simply parts of the same "elephant" is to willfully deny their unique and often opposing distinctives.

In an online article, James Heidinger walks out the logic behind the theological liberalism of the twentieth century that hijacked most mainline denominations, The United Methodist Church among them. The dismantling of orthodox theology began with the character of God, its trickle-down effect impacting everything from our view of humanity to our understanding of the nature of Jesus Christ. Heidinger writes:

> Liberalism believed that just as Christ differs from other men only comparatively and not absolutely or substantively, neither does Christianity differ from other religions. It is just one, perhaps one of the most important, among the world's various religions, all of which stem from the same basic source. Thus, the church's missionary effort should not aim to convert but rather to promote a cross-fertilization of ideas for mutual dialogue and enrichment. The Christian faith is neither unique nor intended to be universal. Thus, the church's worldwide missionary mandate was denied.[1]

This is the elephant redefined as a chameleon. It will be what we need it to be, abolishing the need for absolute truth. It sounds gracious and accepting, doesn't it? Except that it further diminishes the integrity of not one religion but all of them.

To say that somehow, we've all grabbed our own corner of the elephant is to say that the elephant itself is a donkey on one end and a peacock on the other. To call either an elephant is to misdefine the thing. In the story of the elephant and the blind men, no one is right. This elephant isn't a snake or a tree or a rope or a wall. It is an elephant! The blind men can all be equally wrong, but they can't be equally right.

Truth is not relative.

Sadly, The United Methodist Church, in its haste to be ecumenical, took ecumenism a step too far after joining with the Evangelical United Brethren, and at the 1972 General Conference the church endorsed the concept of pluralism as part of the statement called "Our Theological Task."[2] That statement shifted the emphasis from doctrine to ethics, opening the door to a conditional theology that shifts on the sands of experience, tradition, and reason. It is stunning to think how powerful that one word *pluralism* is, and how detrimental to our denomination. The term *pluralism* was eventually removed from our official theological statements, but its presence has created a ripple effect that continues to this day.

A website that pokes fun at Christian culture once posted a marvelously ironic "news piece" about a pastor being surprised to find out his church has a statement of faith.[3] I suspect the author of that bit was within earshot of our United Methodist conversations. I have had folks ask me, "Who are you to decide what 'orthodox' is?" The same has been asked about Wesleyanism, Methodism, and even truth in general. I hear echoes of Pilate's question to Jesus: "What is truth?" (John 18:38).

In fact, these terms have accepted meanings. Our Articles of Religion define what it means to be United Methodist. Wesley's sermons interpret those articles into practical living. We have a doctrine that reflects the thinking of generations; this is the substance of Wesleyan orthodoxy. It is not purely theoretical, but the kind of religion James discussed—the capacity to serve others without letting the world get the best of us (James 1:27). To allow a nontheological culture to redefine our terms would be foolish, and yet this is the plague that has befallen United Methodism and the root cause of our severe sickness. We have forgotten that we are creedal, doctrinal, and covenantal and that our beliefs are to be lived out for the transformation of the world.

Hear that: *we transform the world, not vice versa.*

Our official documents make it clear that we have a doctrine unique to us as Wesleyans, but the glue that holds us together is Jesus. Our confidence is in Christ. This is why Wesley began these nineteen questions as he did: "Have you faith in Christ?" Until you have faith in Christ, none of the rest of this matters. Likewise, both the Articles of Religion of the Methodist Church and the Confession of Faith of the Evangelical United Brethren Church begin with a confession of a Trinitarian God (Article I) and highlight the role of the Son (Article II). Those foundational articles are grounded in Christ as the exclusive Savior of the world. Those who remain connected must insist on a relationship built on integrity and true accountability around the confession of Jesus as the center of our gospel and foundation of our faith. Likewise, both the Methodist Articles of Religion and the EUB Confession of Faith go on to confess the Holy Spirit and the authority of the Bible. The Holy Spirit proceeds from the Father and Son—one substance, one glory, one eternal God. Likewise, we trust the authority of Scripture, which "contains all things necessary for salvation."[4] This is pure orthodox theology and it roots us in One God, Father, Son, and Holy Spirit, and God's word in the Holy Scriptures. Anyone equivocating on any of these points cannot claim to be a classical follower of Jesus Christ in the spirit of the apostles.

Beyond these orthodox claims, our *Book of Discipline* lifts up several theological emphases that highlight our distinctives as United Methodists.[5] Here are some highlights:

The United Methodist Church celebrates lavish grace—prevenient grace, justifying grace, and sanctifying grace. Our communities are built on grace and we trust Paul's vision of grace, where "we throw open our doors to God and discover at the same moment that he has already thrown open his door to us. We find ourselves standing where we always hoped we might stand—out in the wide open spaces of God's grace and glory, standing tall and shouting our praise" (Romans 5:2 MSG).

The United Methodist Church celebrates holiness, or sanctification. In fact, Wesleyan doctrine can be summed up in two words: *grace* and *holiness*. This is perhaps our best theological contribution to the body of Christ. At its core, United Methodism is about claiming a free gift of salvation then working it out daily with fear and trembling. It is a call to live a holy life.

The United Methodist Church celebrates free will. We refuse any attempt to limit the work of Jesus to only those who are in the "up elevator," and we stand by our right to get saved . . . again.

The United Methodist Church celebrates practical acts of mercy and justice. We are doers of the Word and are committed to service that leads to salvation. (This is a key point: we don't serve for service's sake. We serve for Christ's sake.) We trust in the means of grace and believe God will show up in practical acts of piety.

The United Methodist Church celebrates the sacramental life, specifically baptism and the Lord's Supper. We passionately pursue a personal relationship with Jesus and are not bound by forms of religion, so we see these acts as servants, not masters of our life with Christ.

Wesley also included articles specifically dealing with issues of his day. He addressed the church's relationship with the state, as well as points of Catholic doctrine, like transubstantiation and the marriage of ministers. We can embrace the spirit of these articles while understanding they are not matters of salvation for us, nor are they priorities in our theological task. Our emphasis will always be on Jesus Christ as Lord of all and on the Bible as our authority for faith and life.

When Wesley asks if we have studied the doctrines, he is asking not just if we can pass a test on the information. He is asking, much as with the General Rules, if we have owned them, internalized them. There is a hard word implied by this question: Do you know what you believe? Can you articulate it, and is that in line with what United Methodists believe? If not, have you seriously considered what other place you might live out your faith? Do you understand that this covenant into which you are entering is a two-way street? It not only requires the hierarchy to accept you, but it requires you to accept and live the doctrines by which we operate. Otherwise, connection becomes a farce and your witness loses its potency. Have you studied our doctrines to discern if you can embrace them?

There is a later version of that old story about the elephant that includes another character. A king in possession of his sight eventually shows up to tell the blind men they have got it wrong. Their experience has deceived them. This thing they are describing in various ways is, in fact, an elephant.

And so it is with Christianity and of our expression of it as United Methodists. Someone from beyond has come to reveal to the world the heart of God. He has seen what we cannot see, and has come to tell us what truth is. Or more precisely, *who* truth is. Truth is a person, and his name is Jesus. To believe in Jesus alone for salvation is to be a Christian. Nothing else counts.

---

1 James Heidinger, "5 Marks of Theological Liberalism," Seedbed website, June 19, 2017, https://www.seedbed.com/5-marks-of-theological-liberalism/.

2 *The Book of Discipline of The United Methodist Church 1972* (Nashville: The United Methodist Publishing House, 1972), ¶70, p. 69.

3 "Pastor Surprised to Learn His Church Has Statement of Faith," *Babylon Bee*, August 30, 2016, http://babylonbee.com/news/pastor-surprised-learn-church-statement-faith/.

4 *Book of Discipline 2016*, ¶104, pp. 65–67 and 72–73.

5 *Ibid.*, ¶102, pp. 51–56.

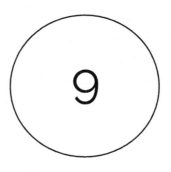

AFTER FULL EXAMINATION, DO YOU BELIEVE THAT OUR DOCTRINES ARE IN HARMONY WITH THE HOLY SCRIPTURES?

Jiro Dreams of Sushi is a quirky little documentary on Netflix about the life of an old man considered to be the finest sushi master in the world. He owns a small restaurant in Tokyo that seats ten people. The wait for a reservation is about a year. He takes incredible care in the seating of the guests and the experience they have of the sushi he prepares. He serves one piece of sushi at a time. Then, he watches his guest eat it to gauge the guest's enjoyment. Critics say the experience is awkward, but the sushi is unparalleled. Every visit, food critics report, is better than the last.

Jiro credits discipline as the secret of his success, and he is radically committed to it. He is relentless in his pursuit of quality—only the best tuna and other ingredients; he seeks the perfection of every element. He is almost machine-like in his work ethic. He never misses a day at the restaurant, even when there are deaths and disasters. Every day, get up and make sushi. Every day, perfect the process. Every day, be obedient to this duty to do this thing.

Jiro would make a great Methodist.

Even in his own meals, Jiro allows himself only the finest of gourmet foods. He limits himself in this way so his palate is optimally sensitized to only the best of the best. In his comments about a French chef he particularly respects, he notes with some envy, "If my palate was as sensitive as his, I'd make even better sushi."

I'm inspired by Jiro. I love his discipline and am struck by that idea of a more sensitive palate. The best sushi master in the world tells me that if I want to be world-class, I shouldn't dumb down the ingredients.

Let me say that again a different way: *If I want to make a difference in this world, I must not compromise the ingredients.*

Brothers and sisters, I believe the United Methodist movement needs a more sensitive palate. In our desire to hold together the widening differences of an increasingly global, increasingly diverse connection, we have succumbed to the temptation to dumb down our ingredients. We have been unfairly influenced by our own poor interpretation of Wesley's maxim: "If your heart is as my heart, give me your hand." In our haste to draft that statement as our banner over the ideal of moderation, we have ignored the context.

The line is taken from the story of Jehu in 2 Kings 10:15, the Scripture text on which Wesley preached his sermon "Catholic Spirit." Through the word of God, Elisha had instructed a young prophet to find Jehu and anoint him king over Israel, giving him the task of cleansing Israel of the unholy influence of Ahab and Jezebel, which had spiritually weakened the people of God (2 Kings 9:1-10). Jehu accomplishes the call with a kind of ruthless calculation that is impressive, if a little startling. On his way to completing the task, he invites a man named Jehonadab to join him for the last leg of his quest, saying, "Is your heart as true to mine, as mine is to yours? (or, "Is it right with your heart, as my heart is with your heart?") . . . If it is, give me your hand" (2 Kings 10:15 NRSV). And with that, they rode together to Samaria where they killed off the remainder of those left to Ahab.

That should have been the end of the story and Jehu's victory lap. His problem was that what he expected of others—a pure and whole heart toward the one, true God—he could not accomplish in himself. He held out a corner of his heart, enough to worship the golden calves in Bethel and Dan (2 Kings 10:29). God affirmed Jehu for his obedience to the call, but made it clear that right actions without a right heart is not the right posture in the kingdom of

God. "Jehu was not careful to keep the law of the Lord, the God of Israel, with all his heart. He did not turn away from the sins of Jeroboam, which he had caused Israel to commit" (2 Kings 10:31).

The point of telling that story is that Wesley's maxim set within its biblical context does not mean what we want it to mean. It is not the story of indifferent tolerance we'd like it to be. It is the story of God's call to holiness and one man's desire (if not accomplishment) to serve the call of God in the company of others as passionate as he. Jehu didn't invite young Jehonadab to ride with him in his chariot because he wanted to make sure everyone was included in the quest. He allowed him to ride because their hearts were in sync.

In other words, this is not a story of compromising ingredients and dulling palates. To the contrary, this is a story about embodying and witnessing to the holiness of God.

I remain convinced that the real issue at stake in The United Methodist Church (as with most mainline denominations today) is how we envision the Lordship of Jesus and the authority of the Bible. What has energetically driven Methodists apart for decades is an inability to unite around John 14:6: "Jesus answered, 'I am the way and the truth and the life. No one comes to the Father except through me.'" Many who serve as United Methodist pastors consider Jesus to be *a* way, but not *the* way. This is neither suspicion nor recent trend. Pluralism has been seeping into our United Methodist tradition since the early twentieth century and is ultimately responsible for all our talk about tolerance and unity. If ours is a one-issue conflict, then it is about how the Word of God (both the person and the Bible) influences all our other choices.

Progressive theology would have us focus on tolerance, yet our core value as Christians is not tolerance but holiness. I become discouraged when I hear the conversation lean toward tolerance and unity as our key values, rather than holiness and respect. As our debates over issues surrounding human sexuality continue to boil, I find myself praying the prayer of the frustrated: "How long, O Lord, how long?" I wonder why we haven't made more before now of our differing views on the nature of Jesus. I hope we have not made an idol of "big tent" structures when God may be up to something else entirely. What if a return to theological integrity is the better move for us all? And what if theological integrity means a smaller tent?

A world of people disagree with our Wesleyan theology on issues like predestination, the exclusive nature of Christ, the authority of Scripture, and the leadership of women, just to name a few. Within our own tribe, there is quite the controversy over the interpretation of Scripture where human sexuality is concerned. This question calls us to examine transparently our own minds and consciences and ask ourselves what we most deeply hold true before we commit to this United Methodist tribe. Otherwise, we find ourselves too quickly frustrated with every disagreement on lesser things. The product of trying to fit a square peg into a round hole is an anxious spirit. But such anxiety doesn't have to exist.

This is where we must be careful to guard our own hearts. I would counsel you with an almost-desperate tone to be honest with yourself about what you believe. Can you answer these nineteen questions and affirm our doctrines with complete integrity? For the sake of our own souls, we must not do as Jehu and get most of the way there but drown in the shallow end. God will hold us accountable for the covenants we make in his name. If yours is not the heart of an orthodox follower of Jesus, and if you can't abide the doctrines affirmed time and again in our *Book of Discipline*, then for the sake of your own integrity, don't set yourself up to commit to concepts you can't live out. I want you to own these doctrines, but if you can't, then for the sake of conscience find a tribe you can live in wholeheartedly.

We can only respond yes to this question of Wesley's when we can answer with complete assurance that our heart is as the hearts of our brothers and sisters through the ages who have lived and died for our brand of faith: Christ alone, and Christ above all, as revealed in the Word of God, our authority for life and faith.

WILL YOU PREACH
AND MAINTAIN THEM?

I have a suspicion.

My suspicion is that this question sits at the center of these nineteen not coincidentally but very much on purpose. For a Methodist pastor (please remember that when Wesley asked these questions, he was asking preachers and not just any preachers, but *Methodist* preachers), this is where the rubber hits the road. After all, Methodism was born out of an approach to life and discipleship that modeled the deep waters of sanctification. That theology resulted in a movement, but it was incubated in one simple question: How do we live this? Wesleyan theology is *practical* theology. When Wesley asks if we will preach and maintain these doctrines, I believe he is asking us this very thing. Will you not only give lip service to our beliefs, but live them out—maintain them—in your daily life and ministry? Will you stand for what it means to be a Methodist-bred Christian even when it isn't easy or convenient?

To that, I personally answer a hearty yes. I was born into The Methodist Church, but the study of our doctrines made me Methodist at the heart level. I believe our doctrines are in line with the Holy Scriptures, and preaching them is my great joy and privilege. I love introducing our approach to theology to those who haven't been widely exposed. But Wesley doesn't ask us here if we will just *preach* those doctrines. He is also asking us to maintain them, to live them in front of others and hold our faith communities responsible for staying the course. That seems to me to be the heart of this question. Not only will you *say* the right things, but will you stay the course year after year, season after season as the winds of culture shift and the moods of people change?

I practice ministry as an orthodox Wesleyan. That means I am theologically conservative and socially active. I preach that Jesus Christ is the Lord of the universe. He is the way, the truth, and the life and no one comes to the Father except by him. I care in practical ways about those who are oppressed, who are being held spiritually, emotionally, or relationally captive, who do not yet know they have the favor of God. I am convinced that holistic ministry means casting out demons, curing disease, proclaiming the Kingdom and healing the sick (Luke 9:1-2).

Holding the line of orthodoxy is difficult in this season. Even if I am committed to engagement with the poor, the oppressed, the marginalized, my position still seems intolerant or unkind to some. To maintain these doctrines in the face of others' suffering draws up arguments about what love is or what justice means. Within myself, I sense the tension but understand how loving God and loving others fits together. Still, I am conscious of the fact that others might experience my beliefs as somehow inconsistent or even hypocritical. And I am not just talking about people in other churches in other towns or conferences or jurisdictions. There is disagreement in my own church (a congregation I planted) about the issues over which our denomination is divided. There are folks in my church who do not want to leave The UMC, no matter what happens. There are people among us who have been hanging on by their fingernails, and who wish we had left—or they had left—years ago. There are people who are considering leaving our church now, because this isn't a fight they care to take up. There are people on both sides of the big issues we face who already left. And of course, there are people who don't really care what happens and wish we would change the subject.

I'm guessing our church is pretty typical in that way. Maybe your church is right there too.

Just as we are, we love each other. My goodness, we do! I am biased, of course, but I happen to believe I serve one of the most loving, healthy congregations around. We are committed to making disciples for the transformation of the world, and these folks are bold in their witness, in their mission, in their community life.

We love each other, and some of us really love The UMC. Granted, that is not all of us. After all, we are a relatively new congregation and most of our folks came to Christ under this ministry. Most of us didn't grow up Methodist. But many of those who came to Christ at our church have also come to deeply value a Wesleyan approach to life and faith. We maintain our doctrines in the way we do life together, so we're passionate about things like sanctification, group life, accountability, recovery, personal and social holiness. While being Wesleyan comes naturally for us, being United Methodist is complicated. It becomes more complicated when we lose sight of the appropriate role of the preacher. My job is not to maintain a neutral stance so everyone can be happy. This is not like a political election, where my opinionating might actually be illegal or immoral. This is about what Methodists believe and this is my charge. I am called to preach and maintain *Methodist* doctrines. To be neutral, to refuse to comment or open the conversation or engage the critical issues, would be spiritual malpractice.

As frustrating as it can be to lead as a United Methodist pastor, I promote this way of life because I am absolutely in love with the Methodist way. I can't explain it, but it is like my mother and my father. The UMC raised me and blessed my call and has given me a place to live out my ministry. And so much more than that, Wesleyan theology gave me a framework for loving God and others that is life-giving. Compelling. Even if denominational politics are so darn annoying.

I remember talking years ago to someone who was once married to a rather grating celebrity, a person who created a lot of controversy. Over the years she had heard all the disparaging comments and had become accustomed to the kind of response I gave when she told me who she had once been married to. I flinched. She had obviously seen that flinch before because she was ready for it. She said, "I am not asking you to understand why I married him . . . but he was my husband, and I loved him."

I was humbled by that. You don't know another person's story. You never know why people hang on as they do, long past what others would tolerate.

In this case, we don't know all there is to know about how any of us comes at United Methodism, social issues, Wesleyan theology. We don't have to understand it, but we are called to listen, to respect one another, to weigh our words, and to take care of each other.

We do so for all kinds of reasons.

Some of us believe deeply in an orthodox interpretation of the Bible, and doing so does not mean we don't love people.

Some of us believe love leads us to affirm and celebrate same-sex marriage, and doing so does not mean we don't love the Bible or have faith in Jesus.

Some of us can sit in that tension with an orthodox understanding of Scripture and be okay with those who disagree, and some of us can't. I need to respect that, and hold it with an open hand.

But at the end of the day, I (like all my United Methodist colleagues) have committed to preach and maintain a specific set of doctrines. I have promised before God and people to learn those doctrines and internalize them, so I can wholeheartedly teach and live them. I don't get to decide what it means to follow Jesus.

Can I just say that again? I don't get to decide what it means to follow Jesus.

Nor do I get to define what it means to be a Methodist. That has already been decided, as has my personal commitment to it.

For whatever it is worth as you wrestle with your own place in the midst of this current storm, here's where I stand. I am the pastor of a community committed to putting Jesus at the center, believing that all people matter and that community is essential to spiritual formation. I want everyone in our church. *Everyone.* I am not afraid of broken people or people who disagree with me; in fact, the more broken the better, as far as I'm concerned. I'm excited by the chance to disciple people, no matter how they come to us. I want to be part of a community of faith where everyone feels radically welcomed and where everyone is radically discipled in matters of faith and life.

Among those who come, I am committed to preaching and maintaining the doctrines of The United Methodist Church as they stand, with particular emphasis on the nature of Jesus and the authority of the Bible. I cannot imagine myself remaining a leader in an organization that continues to allow folks into its leadership who do not agree with our doctrines. Standing in this place creates a remarkable tension that is difficult to maintain, but it would be dishonest for me not to stand in this place. This is where my heart is.

When I stand in this place—compassionate toward people but committed to orthodoxy—my internals match my externals. I encourage you to find that place for yourself where your internals match your externals, so you can preach the Word with passion and maintain the doctrines you have promised to maintain before God and the people called Methodist. The stakes are too high for you to compromise your convictions, and God is too holy to allow you to live a lie.

HAVE YOU STUDIED OUR FORM OF CHURCH DISCIPLINE AND POLITY?

Brazilian artist Tarsila do Amaral was an impressionist painter who used rich colors and unique shapes to capture the message of a nation. As she put it, she wanted to be the painter of her country. I saw her work displayed in the Chicago Museum of Art. Most paintings in the exhibit were displayed as a set, the full-color painting together with a half-dozen drawings and sketches of the same image. It was explained in the notes beside one of the works that Tarsila (as she was known to most) did not release a painting until she had internalized it herself, not just painting it but living it. Studying it. Knowing it.

I'm thinking about that because sometimes these questions seem to repeat themselves, like drawing the same image over and over. Wesley will ask if we know the rules or polity or doctrines, then he will ask what seems to be the same question a different way, and then (as with the doctrines) he may even ask one more time after that. I might know what he is up to. Maybe he wants to know not just if we understand the information, but if we have internalized it, studied it. Do we *know* it? Have we drawn and redrawn the spiritual images conveyed by these ideals, so they are no longer like pictures hanging on a wall that we can ponder and appreciate, but more like lines on our faces or blood running through our veins? Have we not only painted these thoughts but also lived them?

Wesley asks us here if we have studied our form of church discipline and polity. In the next question he will ask if we approve of it, and in the question after that he will ask if we support it. In this repetition, he is calling us to draw and redraw our commitment to the Methodist way until we come to the place where we have internalized it like blood running through our veins. With polity perhaps even more than discipline, our aim is to "own" the spirit of this so we don't run the risk of becoming bitter, book-wielding legalists.

Our structure is designed to create a well-ordered, flexible community. It has done a remarkable job of that for nearly two and a half centuries. Bearing the weight of the second largest Protestant denomination in the United States proves its brilliance. Consider the fact that the core of our discipline and polity was hammered out by a handful of men in the early days, and it is truly remarkable. What they envisioned working for hundreds or thousands continues to be effective for millions. This structure has stood our church well from its fiery days of revival in early America to its current global membership of 12.5 million.

Our polity has proven its ability to flex with the growing (and in recent decades, shrinking) numbers. I am not at all convinced, however, that our historic structure is designed to withstand our current diversity. It may well be that the lack of understanding of this structure has only exacerbated the strain. Surely Wesley did not mean to create a polity (the systems, forms and processes that organize us) that constrained theology while holding churches and pastors captive. And yet, as the denomination has grown increasingly theologically diverse, it has become increasingly difficult to find common ground or solutions that create a sense of confidence in our shared future. This has been our challenge.

Early on in my ministry as a church planter, we had a few folks show up at our church—and one in particular—who were more political than theological about their United Methodism. They had come from dysfunctional United Methodist churches where folks made their point at meetings by bopping each other on the head with *the Book of Discipline* (figuratively speaking, of course). Their passion for treating the *Discipline* like rules in a Monopoly game didn't sit well with folks in our faith community who had come from no church background at all. When we first constituted as a church, probably only a quarter of our folks had any prior experience with United Methodism. Most of the rest (and even some of the United Methodists) came to Christ after they began attending our church. The *Discipline* was more mystery than security for most of those new believers. I took time in newcomer classes to explain in broad strokes the essentials of our structure, but the real beauty of our polity is that when it is working well, it isn't highly visible. It serves the organization without being heavy-handed.

Meanwhile, a militant Methodist among us continued to wield his knowledge of church polity at every meeting, though it rarely had relevance. I remember him being deeply bothered by the fact that we weren't structured more like the church he had come from (a church which had also bothered him, but for other reasons). He didn't like that I took responsibility for the financial health of our congregation (however, exactly as prescribed in our *Discipline*), probably because he didn't like that the pastor knew how little he gave. There were a half-dozen other things he didn't like as well. As a church, we were being structured for effectiveness, and everything we did was "organized to beat the devil," as Will Willimon has said of United Methodists.[1] We had a pragmatic structure that worked, but we were not overly organized. We liked our ability to flex as we grew, and the United Methodist structure allowed for that.

But you know how it is with some folks. For some folks, everything is politics. Our friend called a meeting so he could school us in all things Methodist. He brought a *Book of Discipline* for everyone attending. When we got there, he laid his *Book of Discipline* in the middle of the table and prepared to begin his lecture. But before he started, our lay leader picked up his Bible and set it on top of the *Discipline*. Before he had even said a word, that visual made a powerful statement. "You know, I may not know everything your book says but I know what mine says . . ." I believe Wesley would have approved of that move. We are first of all people of the Book, and that book is the Bible.

Let me state for the record that I believe in our Methodist system. I stand by the *Book of Discipline* and have been incredibly grateful for all the ways it has guided us in ministry. As a church planter, I have been stunned over and over to find that all our creative questions have already been addressed in one paragraph or another. It is a great guide and coach for the church, and it has helped us "organize to beat the devil."

But the *Discipline* was never meant to be our Bible, and our adherence to it was never meant to outstrip our devotion to Christ. The *Discipline* is a servant of the church, not a master of it. Wesley stated this outright. He wrote to John Smith, "What is the aim of any ecclesiastical order? Is it not to snatch souls from the power of Satan for God and to edify them in the love and fear of God? Order, then has value only if it responds to these aims; and if not, it is worthless."[2]

Polity exists to serve the mission, not the other way around. Our conferences, episcopacy, itinerant ministry, and forms of ecclesial accountability all exist to serve the cause of winning souls to Christ and seeing them organize for discipleship. If our full allegiance is not to the cause of making healthy, committed followers of Jesus locally and globally, we are missing the mark. It is far too easy in a politicized climate to get wrapped around the axle, to focus too much on salaries, benefits, and systems, and in the process completely miss the spirit of the law. If we are not careful the system can lull us into nurturing the very spirit of religion Paul warned against: "People will be lovers of themselves, lovers of money, boastful, proud, abusive, disobedient to their parents, ungrateful, unholy, without love, unforgiving, slanderous, without self-control, brutal, not lovers of the good, treacherous, rash, conceited, lovers of pleasure rather than lovers of God—having a form of godliness but denying its power. Have nothing to do with such people" (2 Timothy 3:2-5). This was Wesley's great fear. He opened his "Thoughts Upon Methodism" by quoting this passage from Timothy:

> I am not afraid that the people called Methodist should ever cease to exist either in Europe or America. But I am afraid lest they should only exist as a dead sect, having the form of religion without the power. And this undoubtedly will be the case unless they hold fast both the doctrine, spirit, and discipline with which they first set out.[3]

Wesley went on in that same document to call our Methodism a "religion of the heart." He wondered in writing if we could continue, as folks so quickly become self-concerned, increasing in pride and anger. This brings us back to Tarsila's artistic method. Part of her art was internalizing the work before she released it to the world. And part of ours must be the same. Don't go out there until you've internalized the heart of us, until the bones of our system work their way into your bones. Otherwise, you'll run the risk of being either rebellious or legalistic.

Neither is good for the soul—yours personally or ours collectively.

---

1 William H. Willimon, *Why I Am a United Methodist* (Nashville: Abingdon, 1990), 110.

2 John Wesley, Letter to John Smith, June 25, 1746, quoted in Scott Kisker and Kevin Watson, *The Band Meeting: Rediscovering Relational Discipleship in Transformational Community* (Franklin, TN: Seedbed, 2017), 68.

3 John Wesley, "Thoughts upon Methodism (1786)" in *The Bicentennial Edition of the Works of John Wesley*, ed. Richard P. Heitzenrater, vol. 9, *The Methodist Societies: History, Nature, and Design*, ed. Rupert E. Davies (Nashville: Abingdon Press, 1989), 527.

DO YOU APPROVE OUR CHURCH GOVERNMENT AND POLITY?

I was in my first semester at Asbury Seminary, and I was having a tough time. Really tough. I was not a natural student, so being back in school was a challenge. After ten years away, I had to relearn the discipline of study. All that reading, all those papers! By mid-semester I was ready to give up. I just didn't think I had it in me to live out my call to ministry if living it out meant finishing a master's degree.

About that time, a musician named Dennis Jernigan came to campus to give a concert. I didn't recognize the name, but I went to the concert anyway and I sat in the balcony and listened. Toward the end of the concert, he did a kind of altar call during one of his songs. I found myself at that altar begging God to get me out of this . . . out of seminary, out of my call, out of all of it. I told him, "God, I will do anything. I will suffer any amount of humiliation. Just get me out of here."

I count that moment as one of the genuinely charismatic moments of my life. Just then, the Holy Spirit washed over me and I heard the Lord speak. He said, "I will write the wisdom on your heart."

Now, remember, I was not the brightest bulb in the seminary box. I had no idea at the time that God was quoting Scripture to me. I didn't know yet that the prophet Jeremiah recorded these words of God: "I will put my law within them and I will write it on their hearts; and I will be their God and they shall be my people. No longer will they teach one another [no teachers, no schools!] or say to each other, 'Know the LORD,' for they shall all know me from the least of them to the greatest" (Jeremiah 31:33-34 NRSV). I had no idea that was in there that day when I was just a puddle of self-pity at that chapel altar.

But I knew this: With that word from the Lord I knew I had a real answer to prayer. I had a promise. God made a covenant with me that day, and I believed it. I don't know how long I stayed there at that altar, but it was a long time. My hands were in the air and tears were streaming down my face as I tried somehow to say thank-you to this God who is so merciful and good that he would make that kind of promise to an ordinary person. It blows my mind still to think of it. To think of the God of the universe making a covenant with me, using the very words he first uttered six hundred years before Jesus, brings me joy and amazement. God's words prove that God cares so much about his relationship with souls that he would come all the way down to the altar in our hearts to make promises he plans to keep—promises signed with the blood of Jesus Christ.

This is what God did when he sent Christ into the world. God took the laws and commandments he had written down for the people of Israel back in the days of Moses and put them into the person of Jesus Christ. Then God promised all people that anyone who took Jesus Christ into themselves would have these laws in us, in our minds and written on our hearts. That is the nature of the covenant relationship with God through Jesus Christ. It transforms us because the Holy Spirit possesses us as God's law changes us.

Hannah Whitehall Smith says it is our nature to rebel against laws that are outside of us, but we embrace that which springs up from within.[1] And it is true, isn't it? We always like our own ideas better than other people's ideas. God knows this about us, so God's way of working in us is to get possession of us—to make God's ideas our ideas. This is why Paul could say with confidence, "Christ *in* you, the hope of glory" (Colossians 1:27, italics mine). Without the indwelling Christ, we are just another human being who knows the rules.

That difference between head-level rules and heart-level rules is the difference between life and death in ministry. Just as knowing the law but not owning it was death for the Israelites, so too it is death for us. We are designed for a religion of the heart. There is something to be said for signing on at the heart level, for embracing first our theology, then our polity, and allowing them to shape us from the inside out. We may not approve of every "jot and tittle," but we can affirm the spirit of our tribe. In fact we should affirm this spirit if we are going to be part of this connection.

Let's be honest. No job is everything we love and nothing we don't. Every job has its pluses and minuses. I didn't come into United Methodist ministry because I fell in love with its discipline and polity. I came into the ministry because I love Jesus, and I sense that within The UMC's system of connection and covenant I can serve him well. I complain with the best of them about charge conference and end-of-year reporting, but I manage to accomplish those tasks because they are part of a bigger ministry life that I love dearly. I love healing prayer and preaching and the stunning miracle of seeing someone embrace Christ. I love seeing people get filled with the Holy Spirit. I love the countless hours spent listening and praying, and I love thinking strategically about how to extend this work as far as possible. At its best, United Methodist polity and discipline serves these other causes well. I am well aware that polity is not a matter of salvation, but I know that supporting and maintaining it is the only way our connection and covenant will function. If we all pick and choose which parts we like and which we don't, it won't work. Anarchy ensues.

Wesley's practice of repetition in these questions reveals his understanding of human nature. If I didn't know better, I would think he dealt often with ministers who were weak in the spiritual discipline of letting their yes be yes and their no be no. How much confusion is caused by well-meaning people who have not counted the cost before building the house, who have signed on without letting the spirit of our tribe sink into their bones? Can I say this with complete respect and love? You don't get to decide what it means to be United Methodist. That has already been determined. Any decision to change that must go through proper channels, covered with massive amounts of prayer. Do you approve that? Can you approve the spirit of our discipline and polity while maintaining a generous heart?

Obviously, I made it out of seminary with a degree because here I am as a pastor. To my absolute surprise, I found myself back in school a few years ago completing a doctorate. In our first session together, my doctoral cohort tackled a ropes course. One of our challenges was a two-wire exercise. The wires, about three feet above ground, were stretched between two trees. As they traveled from one tree to the other, they gradually spread apart from each other. One person balanced on one wire and a partner balanced on the other wire. Our task was to lean into one another while we slowly scooted down the wires, even as they spread farther and farther apart. The trick was to lean equally on each other (remember that) as counterweights to hold each other up. It won't work if one leans and the other doesn't, so we both had to lean in and surrender all our weight.

We discovered through trial and error that the best way for two people to scoot down the wire was to listen to each other. We would ask, "What do you need? What does this look like from your perspective? How can I help?" Without verbalizing it, it was hard to know the other person's challenge in that moment. Our teammates on the ground were also there to tell us what we couldn't see. They would say things like, "Straighten up! Push in!" And I'd think, "I *am* pushing in!" when evidently I wasn't. It was almost impossible when I was wobbling on that wire to know my own position. It took all of us working together to get two of us from one tree to the other.

The moral of the story, of course, is that we need each other. This is the point of our connectional system. It is designed for people who trust each other enough to lean in. But it only works if *everyone* leans in. It won't work if one leans and another doesn't. The key to the whole system is vulnerability. It is in keeping my heart soft toward the people God places in my path so that they become the priority rather than the institution. The clearest way I've seen to maintain vulnerability is to speak honestly out of my own experience, even my own brokenness. The man Jesus healed who said, "One thing I do know, that though I was blind, now I see" got a mention in the most-read book of all time (John 9:25 NRSV). The father who said, "I believe; help my unbelief!" is my favorite unnamed person in the Bible (Mark 9:24 NRSV). Both displayed the heart of flesh necessary for spiritual connection to happen.

As you make your own personal inventory of what you believe about our polity and discipline, ask yourself if you are sufficiently healed and whole to lean in—to give yourself wholeheartedly to a connection of Christ-followers who are bent on spreading "scriptural holiness over the land."[2] This is the great need. It is for people ready to partner in both covenant and connection for the sake of a lost and hurting world.

---

1 Hannah Whitehall Smith, *The Christian's Secret of a Happy Life* (Boston: Willard Tract Repository, 1885), 47–48.
2 "Minutes of Several Conversations between the Reverend Mr. John and Charles Wesley and Others," in *The Bicentennial Edition of the Works of John Wesley*, ed. Richard P. Heitzenrater, vol. 10, *The Methodist Societies, The Minutes of Conference*, ed. Henry D. Rack (Nashville: Abingdon, 2011), 845.

WILL YOU SUPPORT AND MAINTAIN THEM?

Awakenings start with prayer; they are the work of the Holy Spirit. The Second Great Awakening in the early 1800s was about evangelism and the character of people's hearts. The revivals in Wales (1904–1905) and at Asuza Street (1906–1915) were about repentance, fasting, and prayer.

The first Great Awakening was about being born into a new family. It was a spiritual renewal that started in England and swept through the American colonies in the 1730s and 40s. The seeds of this awakening were planted on a college campus in Oxford, England, when several students decided to find out what would happen to their faith if they held one another accountable for being spiritually disciplined. It was called the Holy Club. A number of the core members of this club went on to become significant contributors to the world, among them John Wesley, who became the founder of Methodism; Charles Wesley, who would go on to write six thousand hymns; and George Whitefield, who became a famous evangelist in America. After finishing school, Whitefield became an Anglican priest but never settled in one church. Instead, he became an evangelist and preached all over England. In 1740 he traveled to America and preached a series of revival messages that sparked a spiritual awakening. In one year, he traveled five thousand miles and preached 350 times. His preaching was based on one question: "What must I do to be saved?" He answered his own question by preaching justification and new birth.

This was the message of the Great Awakening, which led to a powerful spiritual shift that swept through Europe and then America in the 1700s. Some historians say that this theological shift created the environment that led to the American Revolution, as people began to experience themselves as active participants in the work of God. The spiritual shift that blew the church out of the water was a shift from religion to relationship. It was like people who had been in church their whole lives heard for the first time that they had a deep need to be redeemed by Jesus Christ.

Whitefield preached to tens of thousands of people. He was undisputedly the father of the Great Awakening in the 1700s. Truth be told, they say he was a better preacher than John Wesley. So why is it nearly three hundred years later that we call ourselves Wesleyans and not Whitefieldians?

Kevin Watson, United Methodist theologian and historian, asked this question in his study of the Methodist revival and the first Great Awakening, two movements that rose up together but eventually diverged.[1] Watson says Whitefield recognized even while he was alive the difference between his revivals and Wesley's movement. It was the network of class meetings and Wesley's insistence that new Methodists be thoroughly organized for discipleship. Whitefield once said, "My brother Wesley acted wisely; the souls that were awakened under his ministry he joined in class, and thus preserved the fruits of his labor. This I neglected, and my people are a rope of sand."[2]

Wesley's wisdom was in the development of a discipleship system that joined new and awakened believers to one another for the purpose of mutual support and spiritual care. That one choice allowed Methodism to spread wildly. From 1776 to 1850, American Methodism grew by leaps and bounds. In 1776 Methodists made up less than 3 percent of the American population. By 1850 one in three Americans attending church was Methodist. Hundreds of thousands of people came to Christ in that time, and every single one of them was asked to join a class meeting. That did it.

There was nothing magical or mystical about the class meeting. It was a simple matter of living out what the first believers lived according to their story in Acts 2:42: "They devoted themselves to the apostles' teaching and to fellowship, to the breaking of bread and to prayer." There in eighteen words is the spirit of Christian community. It was not just good Bible study or good fellowship. Those first believers were not trading information without being in each other's lives. This verse gives us a prescription for whole-life discipleship, and this was the model Wesley adopted for his movement. It was a network of groups dedicated to supporting each person's journey with Christ.

And this is how we support and maintain the heart, the soul of our polity. It isn't by knowing the rules and being able to quote paragraph and sub-paragraph of the *Book of Discipline*. It is by becoming active participants ourselves in the work of being a disciple who makes disciples within the context of community. The heart of a United Methodist is whole-life discipleship.

Since the inception of our church, we have emphasized our mission: to make healthy, committed disciples of Jesus Christ for the transformation of the world. But it has only been in the last few years that I've come to understand how my own internal posture has worked against that. I have said I wanted to make disciples, but I have measured our success numerically. And I didn't even go by the right numbers. I counted heads on Sunday mornings, but quietly devalued the number of people in groups. This is typical of pastors. We make it all about Sunday's attendance. We ask each other in the hallways of annual conference, "How many are you worshiping now?" When we have a big Sunday in terms of attendance, we find subtle ways in our online posts of making sure our colleagues know it.

This is not the system Wesley is asking us to support and maintain. The system he built, which changed the face of a young nation, was a discipleship system rooted in class and band meetings. Recall Wesley's words about the value of class meetings:

> It can scarce be conceived what advantages have been reaped from this little prudential regulation. Many now happily experienced that Christian fellowship of which they had not so much as an idea before.

They began to "bear one another's burdens," and naturally to "care for each other." As they had daily a more intimate acquaintance with, so they had a more endeared affection for, each other. And "speaking the truth in love, they grew up into Him in all things, who is the Head, even Christ; from whom the whole body, fitly joined together, and compacted by that which every joint supplied, according to the effectual working in the measure of every part, increased unto the edifying itself in love."[3]

What happened in an early Methodist meeting? In a word, accountability. Conversation began with a question that has come to define Methodists ever since: "How is it with your soul?" This isn't a "How are you?" question. It is meant as an invitation to share transparently around what Jesus is doing in our lives and how that impacts our spiritual development. Those early meetings were about "watching over one another in love." Wesley would say that "if the class meeting was threatened, then the 'very root' of Methodism itself was in danger."[4] These meetings were about transformation, not merely information. As Kevin Watson says, "Early Methodists were asked to invite others into their lives and to be willing to enter deeply into the lives of other people so that together they would grow in grace. They were committed to the idea that the Christian life is a journey of growth in grace, or sanctification. And they believed that they needed one another in order to persevere on this journey."[5]

Wesley died on Wednesday, March 2, 1791. He was eighty-eight years old. They say that as he was laying there, people would come to see him and he would grab their hands and say, "Farewell, farewell." And at the end, with his last breath he cried out, "The best of all is, God is with us," And then he lifted his arms and raised his feeble voice again, repeating the words, "The best of all is, God is with us."

When we commit to support and maintain the discipline and polity of our church, not as a matter of law but as a matter of heart-level discipleship, we can together with Wesley more confidently proclaim that God is with us.

Doctrine, spirit, and discipline together must be the three-stranded cord that holds our tribe together. To bind these three strands together, the

Discipline must serve Scripture, must serve the Great Commission, must serve the great movements of the Holy Spirit. And our fervent prayers must always be that we as a body are spiritually flexible, so we don't miss God's best.

1 Kevin Watson, "The Heart of the Methodist Revival," *Good News*, November 12, 2014, https://goodnewsmag.org/2014/11/the-heart-of-the-methodist-revival/.

2 Conversation between George Whitefield and John Pool, quoted in Holland Nimmons McTyiere, *History of Methodism* (Nashville: Publishing House of the M.E. Church South, 1888), 204.

3 John Wesley, Letter to Vincent Perronet, December 1748, http://wesley.nnu.edu/john-wesley/the-letters-of-john-wesley/wesleys-letters-1748/.

4 Kevin Watson, "The Early Methodists Watched Over One Another In Love," Seedbed website, March 22, 2016, https://www.seedbed.com/the-early-methodists-watched-over-one-another-in-love/.

5 Ibid.

14

WILL YOU DILIGENTLY INSTRUCT THE CHILDREN IN EVERY PLACE?

As much as I love my daughter and as much as I wanted to be the primary influence on her life in her formative years, I am most grateful that from the church she learned to love Jesus. She learned to love by being in the family of God. The church shaped Claire Marie for life and ministry. She learned what it means to be in close and healthy community with other people, and she learned how to love the ones who are hard to love. (Of course, none of the hard-to-love ones went to *our* church, but I'm sure we met them along the way at someone else's church.)

My daughter, an only child, would say she was raised in a large family, and she would be right about that. The church of Jesus Christ is a spiritual family gathered under the loving care of our good Father and under the leadership of the Lord Jesus, our brother. Though the Bible refers to us only a few times in those terms, it is clear the early followers of Jesus saw themselves in this way. God is called "Abba" (Father) by Jesus himself, and in his letters to local churches Paul writes to his brothers and sisters in Christ. If the Bible is any indication, we are family.

The point of growing together as a family isn't to meet together for meeting's sake. Families don't gather so they can say they all sat in the same room once a week. Families gather to do life together, to share in each other's joys and to encourage and call out the best in one another. The point is to be prepared for the work of mission and the formation of souls. It is for children to have parents and spiritual elders they can honor, and for parents not to exasperate their kids through guilt and shame but to raise them up in the Lord. Family elders want their children to surpass the generation before them. I want my daughter to be a better wife, a better mom, a better spiritual leader, a better giver, a better minister of the gospel than I am.

Most of the spiritual formation that happened in our home was caught, not taught. Claire Marie saw her parents pray together every day. At night, she heard us pray specifically for her and over her future. She was always invited into that prayer time. Sometimes she refused it, but most times she was in it. She learned to pray out loud in our home, and she learned that worship and discipleship was a nonnegotiable. We required church and youth group attendance for our child, and she was always around when we held small group meetings in our home. She knows more about the world than I, but less about sin. That's how I would want it for your children too.

Because the family is the basic unit in the kingdom of God, the home matters. If we diligently instruct the children "in every place," that must include especially the home. By answering yes to Wesley's question, we are committing not just to developing a good children's ministry at church, but to training parents to raise their kids spiritually. This was Moses' command to the Israelites just after he uttered what are arguably the most powerful words of the Old Testament: "Hear, O Israel: The LORD our God, the LORD is one. Love the LORD your God with all your heart and with all your soul and with all your strength" (Deuteronomy 6:4-5). After teaching the children of God that their grand design is to love God wholeheartedly, he then immediately instructed them to pass on all God's commands to their children. "These commandments that I give you today are to be on your hearts. Impress them on your children. Talk about them when you sit at home and when you walk along the road, when you lie down and when you get up. Tie them as symbols on your hands and bind them on your foreheads. Write them on the doorframes of your houses and on your gates" (Deuteronomy 6:6-9).

Talk about them as you walk along the way. Moses paints a picture here of a kind of organic spiritual formation that is more caught than taught. This isn't an organized children's program (which is not to say that organized instruction isn't an important piece of the puzzle). This is about teaching parents and other adults how to talk about spiritual things in such a comfortable voice that it becomes a way of life. Not just in Sunday School, but in Starbucks. Not just with curriculum, but conversation. Not just through programs, but while you're making pancakes.

Talk to your children all along the way. Don't talk about God only when they are little and love sitting in your lap while you read from a kid's Bible storybook. Don't talk about God only when they get in trouble as teens and you need them to understand that there are consequences and there is a hell. Talk to your children at the dinner table and in the car, as you watch movies together, and when current events warrant theological positioning. Make the talk of God into something normal and natural so that when the crisis hits the conversation can be comfortable.

This is the first call of a pastor when it comes to families. The pastor is to be a strong spiritual coach for parents, giving them the tools they need to raise up a generation of Christ-following disciples.

My daughter and her husband are leaders in a youth ministry. She tells me she often asks kids, "Why do you think your parents took you to church?" When she asks that question, she almost always gets one of two answers. Some kids say, "Because my parents wanted me to be raised in church." Others answer, "Because my parents wanted me to have a relationship with Jesus."

There is a world of difference between those two motives. I'm quoting Claire Marie here: "If you just want them to be good people, a worship service one hour a week will not change their worldview. It is a culmination, not the headwaters. It can't all depend on church. It is what they get on the other six days that matters. If you want your kids to know Jesus, you can't outsource it. If knowing Jesus is your motive, then you will begin to care deeply about building a spiritual home." When we as spiritual leaders in the church answer yes to this question of instructing the children in our care, we are also consenting to teach their parents how to lead spiritually at home. We want parents who want their kids to know Jesus, not just go to church.

But this take on Wesley's question—that it means teaching the parents—doesn't let us off the hook for directly influencing the children in our care. It is one thing to be a leader by appointment. It is another thing entirely to be a leader by influence. I got the best parenting advice from a young woman I met in seminary. She wasn't a student; she owned a local bed-and-breakfast. She had cared beautifully for my husband and me when we first got to town, so I was impressed with her. She seemed especially well adjusted and healthy for a preacher's kid. I wanted to know how she didn't end up as one of those PK statistics that rejected Jesus when she left home. She told me, "Because my father lived the same life at home that he preached from the pulpit." I made that one line the core value of my own parenting. Whatever mistakes I made (and I made plenty), I am pretty sure my child got the clear idea that Steve and I believe the gospel all the way through. We have lived it. And what we've done for our own child, I am committed to doing for all my spiritual children. My work as an influence continues, because I continue to pastor.

Influence can and should happen intergenerationally in our communities of faith. One of my best days in ministry was being in Starbucks one day and seeing a youth leader at one table with a student and another church member at a table with a student she had agreed to mentor. I was at a table with two college students, and there were students at yet another table witnessing all these adults pouring spiritual wisdom into their generation.

No wonder we call this particular place "Starbucks UMC."

Youth and young adults want experienced voices in their life. According to a LifeWay study, 45 percent of unchurched young adults identified the opportunity to receive advice from people with similar life experiences as very important. And, 68 percent of churched young adults identified the opportunity to receive advice from people with similar life experiences as very important.[1] There is no shortage of mentoring strategies online, so there is no reason why your church can't organize folks into simple, healthy relationships that allow the adults in your community to influence the next generation.

Understand that this doesn't happen without intentionality. Develop the system, then practice the system. Remember Kobe's story (and my maxim) and don't be afraid if your first shot at it is a little messy. That's what grace is for.

In his excellent book, *Seven Things John Wesley Expected Us to Do for Kids*, Chris Ritter notes, "No one can ever call you a failure if you help a child discern the voice of the Lord."[2] Helping a younger person to reach his or her potential by calling out what you see in them is an incredible gift. As biological or spiritual parents who follow Christ, we can sow blessings and vision into our children and harvest a great generation. I want to see a generation of prophetic parents raised up who speak life into their children's lives. I want to see adults in our faith communities empowered to speak life over kids. I want the children in your church and mine to graduate from high school with the sense that the best has been called out of them, that even in their worst moments those who cared for them were able to see what God sees.

I want for the kids in your care the same gift you and I received from our Heavenly Father. Even in my worst days, God saw not just who I was, but who I could be. God saw my best and called it out of me. It is that ability to see what God sees in another person and to speak that into them at every opportunity that is the mark of a great spiritual parent. Will you diligently instruct the children in every place? Wesley's point in casting this question is simply that this responsibility belongs to all of us. Inasmuch as we also participated in the baptism vows of the children among us, we are now required to live that out.

Raise up the children in your care so that when they are adults, they don't have to make the same mistakes we made. Will you diligently instruct the children in every place?

---

1 "Have a Mentor; Be a Mentor—The Biblical Model of Mentoring," Lifeway, excerpted from the young adult ministry handbook, *Context*, http://www.lifeway.com/Article /Biblical-model-of-mentoring.

2 Chris Ritter, *Seven Things John Wesley Expected Us to Do for Kids* (Nashville: Abingdon Press, 2016), 31.

WILL YOU VISIT
FROM HOUSE TO HOUSE?

I planted a church as a "parachute drop" (meaning I and my family dropped into a community unprepared for us) about five minutes before social media became a thing. We didn't yet text, and while Facebook may have been popular on college campuses it wasn't the go-to media source for everyone else. My options were radio, postcards, and old-fashioned door-knocking. If I'd started a church just a year or so later, our marketing strategy might have been completely different.

In those days, we did things no church planter would attempt today. One week, a team of about twenty volunteers set up a phone bank, ordered a list of several thousand names and numbers, and called every one of them. We made literally thousands of phone calls, talking to total strangers about where they went to church and what their prayer needs were. It is a testament to the human spirit that most folks were receptive to our calls.

Another time, we knocked on doors in a neighborhood and asked folks to complete a simple survey. I still remember one guy's answer when I asked if he went to church. "Why would I go there?" he asked. "I feel guilty enough already." And then there was the morning we recruited a small army, met at IHOP, and divvied up thirteen hundred packets of flower seeds with our logo imprinted on them. We paired up and delivered those seed packets door to door along with information about the church. In one day, we personally talked to thirteen hundred people. On their doorsteps. I can definitely attest to Mr. Wesley and anyone else who wants to know that I have "visited from house to house."

I can also tell Mr. Wesley and anyone else who asks that if I had it to do all over again, I doubt I would do it that way. Frankly, it makes me a little tired even to think about it. I admit being a little jealous of church planters who can now make full use of the Internet to market a new work. Yet as I write this, I'm also reminded of fruit born from that season. A young woman's family is meeting her at our local airport tonight to bring her home for the holidays. She is an amazing, gifted young woman, on active duty with the US Air Force. She loves Jesus. When I first met her, she was barely seven years old. We knocked on her family's door and gave her mother a seed packet. She invited us in and asked all kinds of questions about baptism. The family hadn't been in church since the youngest was born. They began attending our church on Easter Sunday many years ago, and that little girl eventually received her baptism as the family received Christ.

There are not enough lines in this book to tell the stories of all the ways our lives have since intersected. Through deaths, remarriages, illnesses, crises, joys, accomplishments, we have become bound to each other in true community. I wouldn't trade anything for the fact that this family—and others—are in our church now because of that house-to-house outreach years ago.

In the years prior to planting a church, I served as an associate pastor in a college town. Not too far from our church was a trailer park. One Saturday morning, a group of us decided to put together some jars of beans and rice (makings for a simple meal) to go door-to-door offering grace and prayer. Our timing could not have been more interesting. The day before, all the households in that park (110 trailers) had received eviction notices. The landowner had just sold the park to a developer who planned to raze the park and develop upscale apartments for students. The folks living there were devastated. Most of those trailers were so old that local ordinances prevented them from being moved. Almost every single family would have to walk away and start over.

We had no idea we were walking into that crisis when we made a plan to fill some mason jars and visit house to house on a Saturday morning.

Because we were Christians, they wanted to know what we planned to do about their problem. They implored us to show up to a meeting they were holding to discuss their plight. We had no idea what we were getting into, but that meeting began what would eventually become a highly organized effort to relocate all those families (many of whom were illegally in the country) into living situations that were stable and safe.

"Will you visit from house to house?" Wesley asked. What a loaded question! We have no idea what we're signing on for when we say yes to this one. When we consent to being in the personal space of other people, we can't control where that leads. If my experience is any indication, folks who visit house to house will pray more, cry more, laugh more, and love more deeply. Preachers who visit house to house will preach better, and those who are not preachers will be more effective witnesses to the gospel in their own way.

Once I visited with someone while she was ill. I discovered that she had an unusually strong love for animals, and her home reflected that passion. There were rabbit hutches in the living room, dogs and cats roaming the halls, guinea pigs, hamsters, and birds lounging in various places throughout the house. I was surprised, actually, by how clean everything was given the sheer abundance of wildlife. Clearly, she had figured out the secret of coexistence.

I sat in the living room in a big overstuffed chair for half an hour, talking with her about all manner of things. Then it happened. A pig—a full-grown, regulation-size pig—came loping out from behind my chair, walked across the room, and used a step-stool that must have been placed for just this purpose to climb up onto the sofa. He grunted his way onto the couch, sprawled out, and went back to sleep.

Let me just clarify: a *pig* had been lying behind my chair, and I had been clueless.

And that becomes the lesson of this tale. I am convinced that behind every door is a story and an opportunity we will miss if we don't learn to visit in homes. I'm so convinced of it that I make a point of training our mission teams in how to knock on doors in other countries. When we go to Haiti, we always spend a few days visiting from house to house, offering to pray for people. Far from being the "scary outsiders," we are always—not often, but *always*—

greeted by folks who are hungry for spiritual connection. We have noticed that after years of us practicing this kind of house-to-house hospitality, folks are now excited for us to visit. People will run to meet us when they see us coming. Our teams have prayed over sick children, dying parents, spiritual darkness, financial distress, joblessness, hopelessness, demon possession, and everything in between. I believe these visits are the most productive part of our trips. Why? Because houses crumble, paint chips, repairs break again . . . but the love of Jesus endures.

In outside sales, a salesman develops a list of prospects to work. The way to work a list is to visit with prospects, get to know them, develop a relationship, and understand their needs. That way, when the customer is ready to buy, you're there, you already know the needs and you are already trusted.

I'm not saying that pastoral care is an outside sales job, but I am saying that professionals whose salary depends on "visiting from house to house" understand the value of repeated contacts, of getting to know people, of being there often enough that you're trusted when a need arises. Current, accurate, and hopeful lists of all who are in our church's sphere of influence are a way we can both treasure and mobilize our people.

We sweep our list every year to make sure every member's name and information is current. We pass information along to ministry leaders, so everyone is in the loop as a family's circumstances change. This is the spirit of what it means to "visit from house to house." It means knowing your people well enough that they "feel" known by those in leadership who are responsible for their spiritual care. Likewise, we are sensitive to those who have stepped away from our church. We remove them from our list so they don't accuse us of not noticing their absence or worse "of only being in touch when we want something." When we remove them, we are in touch to let them know we value the relationship and are here should they need anything down the road.

Every week, we pass around a list in our staff meeting and invite folks to choose a few people to visit, pray over, or send a note to. Every week. And while much of our marketing strategy has changed since our early days as a new church, we are still very old-school when it comes to handwritten notes. We send them by the handful, not as a gimmick but as a way of making sure we remember that these are real people we care for and deserve our utmost care and respect.

My father-in-law was a faithful man and great at knocking on doors. He would teach Sunday school at a United Methodist church in downtown Atlanta, then spend Sunday afternoons visiting families in the housing projects a few blocks away. He was a newsman in Atlanta right in the middle of the civil rights era. After the assassination of Martin Luther King Jr., in Memphis, the whole country went on high alert, searching for his killer or the car—a white Mustang—he used to get away. When the car was found abandoned in that housing development in Atlanta, one of the residents who had come to know and trust my father-in-law called to let him know. That tip became part of the case built against James Earl Ray.

This is the thing about visiting house to house. It isn't about making sure all the seed packets get delivered or about making sure all the houses on a street get checked off before the team can go home. Visiting house to house is about knowing people. Surely this is the real question beneath the question: Will you know people? Will you learn to have spiritual conversations in the context of people's real lives?

Will you be there on days when it isn't necessarily convenient, so you can be there on the days when only the presence of Christ in us will do?

16

WILL YOU RECOMMEND FASTING OR ABSTINENCE, BOTH BY PRECEPT AND EXAMPLE?

I am not a victim.

There are plenty of things in this world I can control. Whether I want to admit it or not, I can make all kinds of things happen that will improve my life. I can will myself to exercise, diet, save money, do Bible study. I can even make myself cook every day if I want it badly enough (clearly, I don't).

Though I am not a victim, there are some things that are beyond my control. There are things I can will into existence, and there are things I can't. There are character flaws, sinful inclinations, health issues, and broken relationships I cannot control no matter how hard I try. Sometimes trying seems to make it worse.

Followers of Jesus discovered this principle one day when they were asked to heal a man's child (Matthew 17:14-21). They tried all the techniques shown them by Jesus himself. They put their faith on the line and called on God to act. Nothing happened. Try as they might, they got only frustration. Then Jesus showed up and with a gesture accomplished the healing. Later in a private conversation, they asked him why they couldn't make this thing happen. Jesus said, "Because you have so little faith. Truly I tell you, if you have faith as small as a mustard seed, you can say to this mountain, 'Move from here to there,' and it will move. Nothing will be impossible for you." Then in some manuscripts of Matthew, Jesus adds, "This kind can only come out by prayer and fasting" (Matthew 17:21). These words about prayer and fasting aren't in all manuscripts of Matthew, so some Bible translations include them or similar wording as a footnote. Even so, it seems that prayer and fasting were important to Jesus and his followers, and they were effective. But in this story, the disciples *had* prayed. Clearly, calling on God to heal someone is prayer, right? What did fasting add that prayer didn't?

Fasting is the deep water of the spiritual life. There is a mystery to it that defies definition. There is a discipline to it also. Nothing will cut through our impure motives and unhealthy agendas quicker than this spiritual discipline. It humbles us. It is an act of obedience. It is proof that discipline matters to God. Fasting cuts through our selfishly motivated agendas and allows us to see truth more clearly. Fasting will transform your prayer life. But let me state the obvious: fasting is tough.

No healthy person likes missing a meal. (Side note: if you're someone who misses a lot of meals due to unhealthy body image issues, you probably shouldn't fast.) Combine that with the fact that fasting will put you in touch with your truest motives, and it is no wonder we avoid it so religiously (pun intended). Because the fact is, nine out of ten of my motives stink, and painful as it can be, fasting and prayer together help me face up to that fact in a way that opens me to a higher way of knowing. When my motives are purer, my worship of God is more real, and my prayers are more effective. No wonder the enemy of our souls would rather we find a reason not to fast!

The Greek word for fasting is *nesteia*, which literally means "not eating." But biblical fasting is not just not eating. It is not eating, with a spiritual goal in mind. In biblical times, people often fasted to acquire a spirit of repentance. Daniel wrote, "I turned to the Lord God and pleaded with him in prayer and petition, in fasting, and in sackcloth and ashes" (Daniel 9:3). This was Daniel's way of getting his spirit in line with his circumstances before confessing the rebellion of his people in the following words (Daniel 9:4-19).

People in the Bible fasted to humble themselves, for spiritual direction, to prepare for spiritual warfare, to seek God's presence, to seek revival, to save lives, or to break a bondage. Sometimes they fasted to wake their souls up. In Joel, the Lord encouraged people to return to him with fasting and weeping and mourning (Joel 2:12). Fasting is a way to stoke our hunger for God. Someone has said it is how we "go vertical." Fasting is a way to go vertical again when we've gotten too horizontal, so caught up in the stuff of life that we no longer notice God or default to his power. Fasting reorients us to that priority of God-focused living.

Fasting is not something we choose so much as something that chooses us. There was a season in my life when I fasted most weeks from Tuesday at noon until Wednesday at noon. I can't say that I discovered any deep, spiritual breakthrough in that season, though I learned to love the taste of Communion (that is how I broke my fast on Wednesdays). Once that season of weekly discipline ended, I fasted sporadically and usually with a prayer goal in mind. I learned by fasting in this way that a person can pray without fasting, but one cannot fast without praying As Jentezen Franklin says, fasting without prayer is just heavy dieting.[1] Fasting drives our hearts upward. I often fasted for concerns I had over situations in my congregation or over people who needed a spiritual breakthrough. It wasn't a regular discipline, but that way of approaching this practice has probably been more meaningful for me than the years of weekly fasting.

One year, our church undertook a major project and we called the whole congregation to fast for twenty-one days. While most folks gave up something but not everything, I sensed a call to fast from all food for those three weeks. I count it as one of the two or three most meaningful spiritual experiences of my life. It was definitely not so much something I chose as something that chose me. Fasting releases the principle of Matthew 6:33, which promises that if we seek first the kingdom of God, all our needs will be taken care of. In those three weeks, I learned what it means to long for God as a deer pants for water. Fasting gave me that gift.

How often we fast or what we fast from is up to us. Not everyone can fast from food, but my experience is that food fasts are like the Corvette of this spiritual discipline. Nothing else will take you further or bring you closer or give you more time to dig around in your soul than a food fast. When God's people fasted, they fasted from food, but note that Wesley mentioned both fasting *and* abstinence. If we can't fast for health reasons, we can abstain from things we like for a time. Abstinence is like a trigger. The act of missing a thing causes us to remember why we're abstaining, which sends us vertical. Try abstaining from desserts or coffee as a kind of spiritual sacrifice. Resolve to abstain from television or the Internet to create extra space and time for God. Consider the Wesley Fast, which is fasting from Thursday afternoon to Friday afternoon; or the Daniel Fast, which is fasting from meats, sweets, and processed foods.

The bottom line of any fast is to diligently seek the Lord, but the blessings that follow are God's gift in return. Fasting is not a battle of wills or a contest of endurance; it is about learning greater dependence on God. What is it you really want God to do for you spiritually? For your church? Do you want God to heal your heart? Deliver you from rebellion? Save your marriage? Bring a rebellious or directionless church into alignment with God's will? Do you want to see the Lord make your people hungry again? Fasting is one way to break through the barriers that keep us mired in mediocrity.

I wonder what would happen to The United Methodist Church if the 12.5 million people who call themselves United Methodist would humble themselves and fast for a season? What spiritual breakthrough might we see? What impasse might be leveled? Fasting won't compel God to act, but it might put us in a more direct line with his intentions for his church. Would you be willing to take one day to fast and pray for the future of our denomination? Does our denominational health matter to you to the extent that you are willing to sacrifice for it? Will you call others to join you?

The question of whether we ought to fast has already been answered. We fast because Jesus assumes it of those who follow him. He himself said, "But when you fast, put oil on your head and wash your face" (Matthew 6:17). Notice that he says "when," not "if." For Jesus and his followers, fasting was a normal part of the spiritual journey, something to take in stride, not for show but for a spiritual purpose.

We also fast because United Methodists assume it of their spiritual leaders. We are committed to the means of grace, all the way out to the radical edge of fasting. This discipline will definitely separate the "men from the boys" (so to speak). If you want to be comfortable in your religion, this question ought to be a hint that maybe you are not meant to be United Methodist. But if you're looking for a fresh dose of faith, fasting can unleash the wind of the Spirit like few other disciplines can. It is God's way of saying to you and me, "Come as you are, but don't stay that way."

---

1 Jentzen Franklin, *Fasting: Opening the Door to A Deeper, More Intimate, More Powerful Relationship with God* (Lake Mary, FL: Charisma House, 2008), 36.

17

ARE YOU DETERMINED TO EMPLOY ALL YOUR TIME IN THE WORK OF GOD?

This has been a tough season. A brother in Christ and a man who has had my back in ministry for fifteen years lost his battle with cancer and passed away on Christmas day. Even in his last days, he was still alert and stunningly faithful. We talked for hours one day in his hospital room about heaven and also about the incredible opportunity he had in those last days to speak blessing over his children. Confined to the bed, he was still looking for ways to use every inch of life for the cause of Christ.

My friend, Steve, was always sort of a bulldog, which is why we got along so well (I'm also a bulldog). I've always been grateful for his encouragement to me to stay the course in the tough times. The word *quit* wasn't in Steve's vocabulary, which may be why he made such a great Methodist. Those of us in the United Methodist tradition are a persistent bunch; discipline is our distinctive. In that spirit, my friend took the challenge of becoming a certified lay minister—the first one in our conference—years after receiving his cancer diagnosis. He completed it just months before his death, at about the same time his treatment options ran out. In the notes he left to help me plan his memorial service, he wrote that completing that course and receiving that recognition from our conference was a highlight of his adult life.

One of the questions for a candidate for certified lay ministry within The United Methodist Church is: "Think about what being 'persistent' means to you in your ministry. How will you stay the course? Where will you be able to find support?" This was Steve's answer to that question, which he shared with me:

> I am persistent in my ministry because I am called. To quit the race before crossing the finish line would deny my destiny and the joy of service. I will be held accountable for how I learn and use His gifts...I can choose to ignore them, bury the gifts in the ground, or invest in His work. To stay this course, I must live what I believe. This is the hardest part. To say Jesus is Savior is one thing. To live with others in such a way that the world knows I am His disciple is another. Each day I must remain Christ centered, in the Word, surrendered to His will and go confidently and boldly forward.

Especially for a man heading into his final season of life, this was an impressive answer. How will you stay the course? What will you do when the going gets tough? Is there character enough in your faith to keep you moving forward when times are difficult? Will you still give your time to this—employing all your time in the work of God—when it isn't fun anymore? As if to answer for us before we have a moment to rethink our own resolve, John Wesley once wrote, "Unless God has raised you up for this very thing, you will be worn out by the opposition of men and devils. But if God be for you, who can be against you? Are all of them together stronger than God? O be not weary of well doing!"[1] What a rare honor to know someone who, right up to the line between this world and the next, has not grown weary in well-doing.

One of my personal favorite Bible characters is an obscure guy named Archippus found toward the end of Paul's letter to the Colossians. I've preached and written on Archippus many times, because his brief mention in the Bible fascinates me. He seems familiar in his struggle.

Paul's letter to the Colossians is an appeal to theological integrity and wholehearted submission to the call of God. Paul wants people to give themselves to the call of following Christ, to be faithful in the follow-through and not just the intention. You might argue that this is a consistent theme in all of Paul's letters, but nowhere is it clearer than in his words to the Colossians. He wants them to be true to the God who has been true to them. He wants them to stand, even when the culture threatens to bend them away from what they've been taught. His letter corrects a collection of heresies seeping into their community. Then, toward the end he does his usual, sending greetings and giving personal instructions to a few friends he knows by name.

And that's where Archippus shows up. Paul calls him out right there in the letter, so everyone else can attest to the charge. He does not plan to leave Archippus to quietly stray off into a more comfortable anonymity. He intends nothing less than wholehearted obedience for this guy.

Archippus is mentioned only in this reference in Paul's letter to the Colossians and in his letter to Philemon. There, he is called a fellow soldier. That label places Archippus among those who have served faithfully with Paul, at least enough to deserve mention. We don't know in what capacity Archippus served, though legends emerged after the fact. The Catholic Church claims that Archippus was martyred. He was buried up to his waist, then children were invited to throw stones at him until he died. Another myth puts him in the company of the disciples who were sent out in Luke 10, after the first wave of twelve went out to preach and heal in towns and villages. A different tradition says that he was the first bishop of Laodicea.

Nonetheless, Paul knows him well enough to know he has a call on his life, so he ends his letter to the people of Colossae with this instruction: "Say to Archippus, 'See that you fulfill the ministry that you have received in the Lord'" (Colossians 4:17 ESV). And then he finishes the letter out. "I, Paul, write this greeting with my own hand. Remember my chains. Grace be with you" (Colossians 4:18 ESV).

Clearly, Paul has a concern for Archippus. Somewhere along the line, this man seems to have lost his way. Maybe he started out well but lost his focus, courage, or interest when the going got tough. Or maybe he was sidelined by family problems or illness. Something seems to have stopped him halfway into his work and Paul wants him to hear that being distracted does not disqualify him from the finishing the race. Once God has called a person, that call is not revoked or amended. A call is a call. See to it, Archippus, that you fulfill the ministry you have received in the Lord. Why? Because it is God's call, not yours. And God cares what you do with your life.

Paul ends his letter ominously. "Remember my chains" (Colossians 4:18). It is an interesting follow-up line to that rather pointed instruction to a man who seems to be struggling to maintain momentum. It is almost as if Paul is setting the sights here for the whole audience, not just one man. Here is where he wants them to aim, not for mediocrity or a halfway mark, but for the radical edge. Fulfill your ministry, he seems to imply, even if it leads to bodily harm. Keep pressing in, even when it becomes uncomfortable, or even if you find yourself publicly ridiculed, privately constrained, or constantly stretched. This is what it means to follow Jesus. He himself said so. "Whoever wants to be my disciple must deny themselves and take up their cross and follow me" (Matthew 16:24). Or what about Jesus' example in Luke 14 of the man who decides to build a tower (a rather grandiose thing to build). "Suppose one of you wants to build a tower. Won't you first sit down and estimate the cost to see if you have enough money to complete it? For if you lay the foundation and are not able to finish it, everyone who sees it will ridicule you, saying, 'This person began to build and wasn't able to finish'" (Luke 14:28-30). Getting halfway there did not seem to be a value for Jesus or those who followed him. To the contrary, Jesus had pretty harsh things to say about those who were lukewarm (Revelation 3:16).

This is a fact: We have been called to be inconvenienced for the sake of the gospel. I know this, because I can't find anything else but those kinds of stories in the Bible—stories of apostles and the widow with a penny to her name and John the prophet who sat on an island alone to write hope to the churches in Asia. All of them are stories of people being stretched beyond themselves toward the kingdom of God and they all teach the same lesson that God has not called us to be comfortable; he has called us to be great. As we follow, we find ourselves more and more in the company of the brokenhearted, the blind, the poor, the prisoners, and even those oppressed by demonic forces.

People who are hungry for healing, and who need spiritual leaders who have the courage to finish what they started, not because they are that bighearted, but because God is that big.

Surely this was the warning embedded in Paul's message to Archippus. It was a warning to hang in there, even when it gets hard. Because the call of God will not lead anyone to more time on the couch or toward popularity or toward wealth. This gospel was designed to lead us toward Jesus.

This is the treasure that meets us at the fulfillment of our calling: Jesus. An authentic call lived out faithfully will always lead us to Jesus.

The word to Archippus is a word to every person who claims a passion for living a Wesleyan expression of faith: Fulfill what you have received in the Lord. Employ all your time in that work. Spend yourself for it. Be wholehearted in that pursuit so that in the end you will have participated in the answer to Jesus' own prayer: "Thy kingdom come . . . on earth as it is in heaven."

---

1 John Wesley, Letter to William Wilberforce, February 24, 1791, http://wesley.nnu.edu /john-wesley/the-letters-of-john-wesley/wesleys-letters-1791/.

18

ARE YOU IN DEBT SO AS TO EMBARRASS YOU IN YOUR WORK?

I have a friend who tells me her biggest fear where I'm concerned is that when I get to heaven, Jesus will greet me with the words, "It wasn't funny, Carolyn." I hope she is wrong but I get how it could happen. I suspect I think a lot of things are funny that probably make Jesus cringe.

Debt is not one of those things. Debt is not funny. Which makes it ironic that when these nineteen questions are asked of ordinands in the opening pastor's session of our annual conference, this one always evokes a wave of nervous laughter. It isn't debt that makes us laugh, but that evidently it takes a lot to embarrass some pastors.

Too many of us have lost our sensitivity to irresponsible living. It begins, for many pastors, long before we enter the ordination process. We roll our college debt into our seminary debt, then find ourselves at the low end of the salary scale when we enter our first appointment. Children, cars, vacations . . . it all adds up, and every year we find ourselves a little further behind. Some also carry the crushing weight of poor decisions made in the days before we came to Christ or found our calling. We feel this tension between our responsibilities and our desire to live a life comparable to the folks in our spiritual care. We sing, "I surrender all," and mean it with our whole heart, but some days it seems like we've surrendered more than we have to give. That nagging desire to be out from under the weight of debt hangs in the air like a cloud and creates stress fractures in our relationships and even in our integrity.

Are you in debt so as to embarrass you in your work? That question presses us at the point of our very identity. What really matters to us, and how much are we willing to sacrifice for this call?

Do you remember the story of Simon, the guy the disciples met after they began to preach in cities around Jerusalem? His story is told in Acts 8. Simon evidently had impressive gifts and was popular with folks who heard him preach. He was called a sorcerer; he channeled supernatural power. When he heard Philip preach in Samaria, he was so taken by the message that he believed, was baptized, and began following Philip around. When Peter and John laid hands on some other new believers so they would be filled with the Holy Spirit, Simon was there and was impressed by that display. That infilling of the Spirit pricked an old ambition. Simon had a thing for power. He went to the disciples, pulled out his wallet, and offered to pay for a dose of what they had. "Give me also this ability so that everyone on whom I lay my hand may receive the Holy Spirit" (Acts 8:19).

Peter was indignant. "May your money perish with you, because you thought you could buy the gift of God with money! You have no part or share in this ministry, because your heart is not right before God" (Acts 8:20-21). Simon almost had them fooled—almost had himself fooled, even—until he pulled out his wallet. In that one smooth move, he revealed his heart. I'm convinced this is a universal truth: the health of our relationship with God is revealed by our relationship with money. This is why anyone embracing spiritual leadership must first deal with their own money issues first before they can lead others. It is also why pastors must be unashamedly interested in how their people relate to money. Our *Book of Discipline* charges elders and local pastors with stewardship of a church's giving records, for the purpose of pastoring people at the point of their finances (par. 340.2.c). This isn't about us; it is about God, who demands our undivided allegiance.

Somewhere along the way, I heard about a billboard advertising an illicit dating service that reads: "Life is short. Have an affair." I suspect a slogan like that works because it taps into something inside us that privately fears life is passing us by. We buy into the lie that life is short and in our impatience to find significance, we grab for what we can touch and control. In the process, we lose what is most valuable. For a visual on this, reread the story in Acts 8. This was Simon's downfall. He bought the message of Jesus, but never cut off his love affair with money and power. I wonder how many pastors are quietly subverting their own ministry because they can't quite let go of their love affair with all the things money can buy?

When Steve and I got married, we were not practicing Christians. Tithing was not part of our life for the first few years of our marriage. When we became followers of Jesus, we started doing what most people do. We dropped a twenty in the plate most Sundays. We were probably giving about 2 percent of our income to the church and to be honest, we felt good about that. We were renters with credit card debt and owed on two cars, so giving anything was a stretch for us.

Then a man named Sam, whom we both respected a lot, stood up in church one day and talked about the time Jesus said, "Give and it will be given to you, a good measure pressed down, shaken together and running over" (Luke 6:38). He talked about how his dad, a rural storekeeper, would sell grain and how the farmers would tell his dad, "You give good measure." Sam told us about a Sunday school teacher who once told him, "You will never be all you are supposed to be until you begin to tithe." He asked her what exactly she meant by tithing and she said, "Ten percent. Tithing is giving 10 percent of your income back to God. It is an act of faith." Then Sam asked the question we all wonder about. "Is that 10 percent of my gross income, or net?" She said, "Gross." From that day on, Sam tithed off his gross income and he said that he discovered that as he gave, it was given to him—a good measure, pressed down, shaken together and running over. Just like Jesus promised.

We heard Sam's story in church one Sunday and when we got home, Steve said, "Carolyn, I think we ought to do it. I think we ought to give 10 percent." I told him it wasn't possible. I reminded him of our circumstances. We were renters. We had credit card debt. We owed on two cars. We were barely scraping by when we gave 2 percent. It wasn't possible to give more. I argued reasonably with Steve along these lines, but when you're talking regular math to a man doing Kingdom math, something gets lost in the translation. Finally, I gave up. I figured, when we ended up with more month than money, he would get it.

In one week, we went from being tippers to tithers, and I know it isn't supposed to happen this way (and I get the danger of telling our story just the way it happened), but this is how it happened for us. We gave, and it was given to us: a good measure. In the nearly three decades since we started taking God at God's word, everything we have needed, we have had. We are not wealthy by any standard, but we have learned that the Lord provides and we have never lacked. Giving is how we became debt-free but much more, giving is how we gained the heart of a giver.

This is the moral of the story: the tithe is how we got past the lie that life is short and into the truth that life is designed to be eternal. Giving helped us live into our created design. We are made in the image of God, and God is at the very core a giver. God, who is a giver, invites us into an eternal perspective where all that God values is ours. Isn't this the point of the father's statement to the older son in the story of the prodigal? "My son . . . you are always with me, and everything I have is yours" (Luke 15:31). So much of debt is our way of expressing doubt in the truth of that statement. Rather than trusting God to celebrate over and provide for us, we play the prodigal and grab for our own power and provision. It didn't work then, and it doesn't work now.

Are you so in debt as to be ineffective in your leadership? Does your relationship to money compromise your message of trust and surrender? Here is your remedy: become a giver. Deeply, from the heart, learn to give cheerfully and generously, and watch God transform your relationship with money.

Brothers and sisters, you will never be all you are supposed to be until you conquer your debt, release control of your finances, and begin to give from a generous heart.

WILL YOU OBSERVE
THE FOLLOWING DIRECTIONS?

(a) Be diligent. Never be unemployed. Never be triflingly employed. Never trifle away time; neither spend any more time at any one place than is strictly necessary. (b) Be punctual. Do everything exactly at the time. And do not mend our rules, but keep them; not for wrath, but for conscience' sake.

All. In the right context, that little three-letter word can be dynamite. In Paul's second letter to Timothy, he uses those three letters to galvanize the energies of a young evangelist. Mentoring his young friend, Paul acknowledges that not everyone will serve this gospel faithfully. Some will not put up with sound doctrine. They will become keepers of the myth rather than carriers of the gospel. In a burst of advice, he writes, "But you, keep your head in all situations, endure hardship, do the work of an evangelist, discharge *all* the duties of your ministry" (2 Timothy 4:5, italics mine).

That little word *all* in the midst of this charge ("discharge all the duties") reminds me of the fine print at the bottom of a job description, the one that says, "other duties as assigned." You don't find out until you take the job that the "other duties as assigned" take about forty hours of your workweek.

What Paul is trying to tell his first-century audience and also us is that ministry is a package deal. It is not just the "glamour shot" moments, the joy of preaching an inspiring message or the honor of being asked to speak in big venues. It is not just baptizing new believers or designing a moving worship service. Most ministry happens in the broad daylight of life, when our favorite student gets suspended from school or our dear friend dies before his time. What Paul teaches us, and what Wesley communicates through these final questions, is that the best we can bring to every circumstance—both the joyful and the mundane—is the simple discipline of being fully present. Be present to the work, Wesley teaches us. Be in the right places, on time, with the right attitude, so you can be there when Jesus shows up.

One of my favorite stories of Jesus as a baby is the story of Simeon and Anna. Anna was the prophet who just happened to be walking through the room the day Mary and Joseph brought their baby in to the temple for the ritual blessing. The scene is described in Luke 2. When we meet Anna, she is eighty-four years old. She lost her husband after just seven years of marriage, when they were still young and wide-eyed, with dreams of a houseful of children and a respectable income, a good home near her parents, and a reliable neighbor to visit with while her husband went off to the temple to pray.

She could not have guessed on her wedding day that way too soon she would be the one going off to the temple, as was often the custom for the widows of her day. She would live off its charity and make the best of a bad situation. From the way Luke tells the story, it sounds like she did. She was fully present to the task of a widow at the temple. She became known as a prophet who spent her time praying and fasting and worshiping God. Because she never left the temple, she was there to witness the Messiah when he came.

Sometimes just being there is enough. If you're a baseball fan, you may remember Cal Ripkin. For decades, he has held the record in major league baseball for playing the most consecutive games. He passed Lou Gehrig's record on September 6, 1995, the night he played his 2,131st game. Ripkin has long since retired, but when he was playing ball, he was a good baseball player. He had a decent batting average and was a solid shortstop. But what made him a famous ballplayer was simply the fact that he showed up for work every day.

Sometimes, just being there is enough.

Being open to God's ability to work and being ready to receive God is not as easy as it sounds. In order to "be there" for God, Anna had to keep a steady diet of prayer and worship. The discipline of faithfulness is what made her heart available when opportunity knocked. Because of her faithfulness, when the Messiah presented himself at the temple she was ready. On that day, in that moment when the Christ was before her, she understood it was not so much where she had been or what she had been through, but whether or not in that moment her heart was available to God. This is Anna's lesson for us. It is not so much where you have been or what you have been through, but whether—right here, right now—your heart is available to God.

Take the first two parts of this three-part question in that spirit. Wesley wants to know, first of all, if we are willing to show up day after day and give ourselves to this work without wasting opportunities? Will we be on time, honoring the time of others by being prepared, not wasting time, not showing up when we feel like it while others are made to wait? Will we be prepared enough to be flexible? I love the way Eugene Peterson translates a line in Matthew 12:7: "I prefer a flexible heart to an inflexible ritual." By asking us to be efficient and punctual, Wesley isn't counseling inflexibility, but wholeheartedness. Are you willing to give yourself to this? *All* of yourself? Are you prepared to be faithful to this call on the days when it is more about obedience than adventure?

And then there is a third part to this question. Wesley wants to know if we will keep these rules "not for wrath, but for conscience' sake." In other words, will we be faithful to these rules not because we might get in trouble if we break them, but because we have given ourselves to this work? Will we have the posture toward our work that Paul called servants to have toward theirs? "Serve wholeheartedly, as if you were serving the Lord, not people" (Ephesians 6:7). Taken in this spirit, these three parts of question nineteen are very much the same question: Will you serve wholeheartedly? Will you give this your all?

Let's face it: We don't need any more pastors who can get the bulletin printed, follow an order of worship, and preach three points and a poem. We have met our quota of folks who can fulfill the minimum requirements necessary to hold an appointment. We have more than we need of people willing to sit in on the sidelines of ministry and offer their opinion without getting in there and giving it their all. The church has plenty of observers, but not so many wholehearted followers of Jesus. The kingdom of God is starving for Spirit-filled followers whose hearts ache or for those who are hungry for healing and who are waiting for someone to come who can confidently carry out *all* the work of ministry, whatever it takes.

In *Beyond Hunger*, by Art Beals, there is a story from Senator Mark Hatfield who once toured Calcutta with Mother Teresa. They visited the ministries of the Sisters of Mercy. They visited the "House of Dying" where sick children are cared for in their last days. They visited the dispensary where desperately poor people line up by the hundreds to receive medical attention. Hatfield watched Mother Teresa minister to all these people with very few resources, and he was overwhelmed by the sheer magnitude of the suffering. He asked her, "How can you bear the load without being crushed by it?" Mother Teresa replied, "My dear Senator, I am not called to be successful. I am called to be faithful."[1]

There's the rub. This call to all of ministry is a call to faithfulness. Faithfulness is the foundation of effective ministry. It is what we who serve this church must hunger after. Faithfulness—obedience, wholeheartedness—will call you over and over again to fight past your feelings and hang in there. In Paul's first letter to Timothy he implores him to hang in, to take hold with both hands of this life to which he has been called (1 Timothy 6:12). In other words, Paul says, stick with this. Not just the letter of it but the spirit of it. Keep your word. Let your yes be yes. Be the kind of servant of Christ people can count on.

How do we accomplish that kind of wholeheartedness? Outside of the power of the Holy Spirit, it is impossible. Without the indwelling Spirit, we are setting ourselves up for a rapid and devastating burnout. This is why Jesus told his followers after the resurrection not to step out into ministry until they'd been filled with the Holy Spirit. "Stay in the city," they were told, "until you have been clothed with power from on high" (Luke 24:49). Jesus knew that without the power and leadership of the Holy Spirit, his people would fall headlong into disappointment. "You are not responsible for anything," Jesus would say, "until I come and invest you with the power to do it."

And so they waited. They waited fearfully, doubtfully, questioningly... cluelessly.

They waited while Jesus ascended and the Holy Spirit descended, and then they were shot out into the world to prepare the world for the second coming of Christ. Under the power of the Spirit, they flowed fearlessly out into the streets to share this gift, to give what they had been given. All of it.

This is what I hope and pray for you. I pray that you will be filled with the Holy Spirit and given power to live out *all* the duties of your ministry with joy and authority, whatever those duties may be. I want you to be so sensitive to the movement of the Holy Spirit that you are able to turn on a dime, spiritually speaking. I want you to be wholehearted in your commitment to Methodist theology. I want you to be confident in your beliefs so you can live them unapologetically. I want you to be committed to orthodoxy—the faith of our fathers—and to Jesus as the way, the truth, and the life. I want you to be able and willing to go where he goes. I also want you to stay put until you have received the power of the Holy Spirit, because I know too well that going out there—out from under the cover of the Spirit—is either dangerous or useless. Neither option is good.

What I want for you is what I want for our whole tribe. I long to see a Methodism infused with power: power to love, power to cast out demons, power to cure diseases and heal the sick. I long for a movement so energized by the person and work of the Holy Spirit that the winds of empty doctrine have no power, no voice in it. I long for fearless leaders who peer over the edge of God's promises and see only potential. I want a tribe so passionately committed to Jesus as Lord and the Bible as our final authority that we will stop at nothing to defend what has been entrusted to us.

Brothers and sisters, I so want all of us to be ready for the next great move of God! What do you need to surrender right now, so you can wholeheartedly embrace that next move? So you can participate in the next great move we are all hungering for? What misconceptions, doubts, fears, anxieties, disenchantments are you harboring that threaten to weaken your faith? What prayer of surrender will make you ready to give your all for the One who has given his all for you?

---

1 Art Beals, *Beyond Hunger: A Biblical Mandate for Social Responsibility* (Multnomah, 1985), 9–11.

THE

19

QUESTIONS TO KINDLE
A WESLEYAN
SPIRIT

CONCLUSION

Now the Lord *had said unto Abram, Get thee out of thy country,*
and from thy kindred, and from thy father's house, unto a land
that I will shew thee. (Genesis 12:1 KJV)

This was the version John Wesley was working off of when he wrote his commentary on Genesis. "Get thee out of thy country." That phrase particularly seems to have captured Wesley's imagination. Why would God have a person leave what they know for an unknown, untested future? Command it even? Was it because Abram loved his native land better than God, Wesley wondered? Was he too attached to his friends? Was this a test, to see if Abram could walk away from all he held dear for the sake of obedience to God?

In the story in Genesis, Abram obeys that call and heads off on a journey to he-knows-not-where. Even after he gets out into this unknown land, he will be further tested. In the next chapter, he and Lot must make a choice. Their two families have become too big and unwieldy, so that living in the same valley has become impossible. The herdsmen are becoming impatient with each other and beginning to quarrel (doesn't that sound eerily familiar?). For the sake of keeping the peace, Abram explains, they ought to part ways. Lot heads off toward what he believes is lusher ground, so Abram is left there to trust in God on this foreign soil.

Commenting on the faith required of Abram to follow God's call, Wesley describes it this way:

By this precept he was tried whether he could trust God farther than he saw him, for he must leave his own country to go to a land that God would shew him; he doth not say, 'tis a land that I will give thee nor doth he tell him what land it was, or what kind of land; but he must follow God with an implicit faith, and take God's word for it in the general, though he had no particular securities given him, that he should be no loser by leaving his country to follow God.[1]

Wesley defines faith in this story as the quality of being able to trust God farther than you can see. What a good word for us as we enter a most intense season of deliberation around the future of The United Methodist Church. We are heading into an unknown country. We may sense a direction off in the distance that seems more lush, but there is no guarantee of what we will find when we get there. (Remember how it turned out for Lot? He settled near Sodom, which God later destroyed.) We may be called to leave everything we love and trust behind in order to get to the promises of God. In the face of our uncertainties, can we trust God farther than we can see?

I am embarrassed to admit, actually, just how recently it has occurred to me that I ought to be praying for my own faith, for the character of it and the density of it and the life of it. It just hadn't occurred to me for far too much of my walk with Christ that if faith is all that connects me to Jesus and if faith is the only thing of any value I bring into this vocation, and if I can't conjure it up on my own because even my faith is a gift from God, then I had better start praying for it. I had better get to shaking the gates of heaven on behalf of my own faith, praying for God to give me more of it, to increase my heart for him and to have more of him in my heart.

I'd better start asking to trust God farther than I can see him . . . and then farther still.

Think of it like you're hanging over the edge of a cliff, and the only thing between you and a five hundred-foot drop is a piece of rope you're hanging on to. Don't you think, if that was your situation, you'd become very interested in the quality of that rope? Don't you think you would be really grateful for the guy who was really good at rope-making and for the quality assurance manager who inspected that rope for flaws? If that rope is all there is between you and death, don't you think you would be praying like crazy for that rope to hold?

If I want to see beyond my present circumstances, if I want to detect the great moves of God, if I want to be able to trust what I cannot see, then I'm going to need a faith that will hold me between the high points. If I want to see resurrections, if I want to see streams in the desert, this is the kind of faith I'm going to need.

If the people called Methodist want to see a new day of hope and renewal, we had better learn to trust farther than we can see. We had better begin cultivating and operating from faith in Christ, which brings us back precisely to the place where Wesley would have us begin.

Have you faith in Christ?

This, we said, is what marks us as Methodist. It is what marks us as *Christian*. Faith is the life of Christ living itself out in me. Followers of Jesus are not those who passively wait for things to change while we sit on the sidelines and wring our hands. We are doers. Our faith lives itself out.

We are being called to leave this "country" of contention and division and discouragement we have been in for decades that has resulted only in membership decline, theological confusion, and internal strife, and head toward a land God will show us. Will we trust him enough to go with him on this journey, even if it means radical change? Will we trust God farther than we can see? Will we have faith in Christ, resisting every urge to preserve the institution as we know it while we march toward the promises of God?

A faithful theologian, pastor, and apostle who once led a risky renewal movement that has since inspired countless men and women toward Christian discipleship would urge us to be fearless and faithful with these words: "He should be no loser by leaving his country to follow God."

---

1 John Wesley's Explanatory Notes, Genesis 12, http://wesley.nnu.edu/john-wesley/john-wesleys-notes-on-the-bible/notes-on-the-first-book-of-moses-called-genesis/.

CPSIA information can be obtained
at www.ICGtesting.com
Printed in the USA
LVOW03s1051050418
572358LV00003B/3/P